Lawrence

Modern Masters

Editor: Frank Kermode

Lawrence

Frank Kermode

Fontana/Collins

First published in Fontana 1973
Copyright © Frank Kermode 1973
Printed in Great Britain
by Richard Clay (The Chaucer Press), Ltd,
Bungay, Suffolk.

To Richard Poirier

Contents

Acknowledgments

My thanks are due to friends who have read this book in manuscript and eliminated some of its errors and confusions: Colin Clarke, Denis Donoghue, Brian Finney, Susan Oldacre, and most of all Anita Van Vactor.

Prologue

[*The White Peacock*, *The Trespasser*, *Sons and Lovers*]

This brief account of D. H. Lawrence's voluminous works must obviously not try to say a little about everything. Hence its apparent neglect of the short stories and the poetry. The novels and certain long stories are central. Within these limits there are further restrictions. To do what seems to me the important job—to show how the visionary is contained by the novelist, how the prophetic fury is woven into the silk—one has, I think, to recognise that the problems of the mature Lawrence become recognisable only with the writing, in 1913, of the Preface to *Sons and Lovers*. Reflecting on his book after its difficult completion, Lawrence began a new career; henceforth he was more conscious of his prophetic role, and would have not only to develop it, but reconcile it with his narratives.

It seems necessary, therefore, to treat the early work—though it contains so many premonitions of the later—as a Prologue. In it the early life and work of Lawrence are discussed with a terseness that I hope his admirers will condone. The main business of exposition begins, naturally enough, with Chapter 1.

Lawrence was born in Eastwood, Nottinghamshire on September 11, 1885. His father was a miner, his mother a former schoolmistress who never fully accepted the miner's idiomatic lifestyle, wanting something more cultivated. This ambition deeply affected her children, and especially Lawrence himself, who became her favourite on the death of his elder brother Ernest. The conflict between the mother and father, recorded in *Sons and Lovers*, was crucial for Lawrence, who grew more and more severe on the mother's demands and assumptions; eventually he attacked mother-love with a kind of hysteria, while the father's indifference to what she regarded as finer things, and his natural ability to enjoy himself, seemed more and more attractive. In a late autobiographical fragment Lawrence laments the taming of the colliers in the generation after his father's, and the loss of 'a sense of latent wildness and unbrokenness' matching a countryside which 'had a lonely sort of fierceness and beauty, half-abandoned, and threaded with poaching colliers and whippet dogs'. The next generation of miners succumbed to its mothers, and became 'sober, conscientious and decent ... the men of my generation ... have been got under and made good' (*P.I.* 817–18).* The older miner in his pub left the moulding of his children to his wife, who turned the boys into the kind of husband she herself wanted —docile, well under her thumb. So the dreams and unfulfilled desires of generations of women came to fruition at last, in the women-dominated half-men of Lawrence's generation.

When Lawrence opened *The Rainbow* with an account of the way in which outward-looking, aspiring women changed the life of their contented menfolk, so inaugurating the changes which would come to crisis in the life of Ursula Brangwen, he was thinking of his mother and of the girl Jessie Chambers, the Miriam of *Sons and Lovers*, whose culture and sexual unresponsiveness he treated as evidence of a female sell-out to the bad kind of consciousness. His father, he came to think, was closer to a more vital and joyful way of being in the world.

Lawrence was a sickly child, a little cut off from other boys, and this threw him more in the way of his mother. The extremely vivid sense of landscape and flowers, memorably expressed in both *Sons and Lovers* and *The White Peacock*, he shared with her. But he was affected just

* A key to abbreviations is contained in the Bibliography, pages 148 ff., below.

as deeply by the life of the pit-village, still visible as an interruption in the midst of unspoiled country, and by the intimate knowledge he acquired of the miner's life. From his first tentative stories to his last novel, *Lady Chatterley's Lover*, he went on exploring his complicated feelings about miners; wherever there is a possible place from them—in *The Lost Girl* and *Women in Love*, in stories such as 'Jimmy and the Desperate Woman'—they enter and change the tone of the tale. The miners of Lawrence's youth were, compared with their successors, quite well off; they had not experienced the oppression that came with fuller industrialisation and mechanisation of the pits—an issue that Lawrence deals with at length and with much imaginative force in describing Gerald Crich's takeover from his paternalistic mine-owner father in *Women in Love*, and also in *Lady Chatterley's Lover*. Women played little part in the lives of the old miners, which were divided between the pit and the pub. As a child Lawrence shared his mother's disgust at the father's drinking; he saw it differently later, but the notion of miners as a race apart never left him. Often they seemed creatures from under the earth, their physique distorted by peculiar labours; and their darkness and difference could give them a perverse sexual attractiveness, for example to Gudrun in *Women in Love*. Their wives might long for a piano in the parlour, but they remained mysterious, Nibelung-like figures, even when corrupted by machinery—'weird fauna of the coal-seams ... Creatures of another reality ... Elemental creatures, weird and distorted, of the mineral world!'[1]

It is characteristic of Lawrence that he could hold, to the end, a double vision of the collier, one part mythical, the other founded on everyday experience. He lived with a miner, underwent the torture by teasing when collecting his father's pay, saw at first hand the results of pit accidents, and taught miners' children in the local school. But this did not inhibit the development of a myth. We shall find him

9

always ready to express himself in such dualistic terms. The father is associated with a beneficent though mysterious darkness, the mother with a malefic education and culture; between such opposed tendencies he habitually imagined a third thing, a tension or reconciliation; and in this instance that third force is himself.

Lawrence, obedient to his mother, made good use of the educational provisions of his region. It would certainly be absurd to represent him as under-educated, or self-educated; and although Ford Madox Ford's account of the young people of Eastwood 'talking about Nietzsche and Wagner and Leopardi and Flaubert and Karl Marx and Darwin' or playing Debussy on the piano while Lawrence's father shared out the week's pay (Nehls, I. 151–2) is his usual 'impressionism'—Ford, like other well-born writers, never got over his amazement that a miner's son should have talent— there can be no denying that there was a flourishing regional culture. It was founded on the chapel, the free library, and a flow of visits from great speakers, often exponents of English socialism. It was an age in which regional working-class people felt that they had a right to national and international culture. When Lawrence left Eastwood for Croydon he quickly settled down and became familiar with the metropolitan scene, met authors, went to the theatre and the opera. Wagner, in fact, came to mean almost as much to him as to Forster, a contemporary with whom he has much more in common, despite the class difference, than appears on the surface.

Of the friendships and love affairs of Lawrence's early years it is unnecessary to speak in detail. He was clear that his mother prevented his achieving a stable relationship with another woman. His engagement to Louie Burrows during his mother's last days was some kind of desperate gesture; and the relationship with Jessie Chambers, whether one reads his or her version of it, was obviously overshadowed in the same way. He was attracted, mostly, to very intelligent women; 'Miriam' was a gifted writer, as her memoir of Lawrence proves, and so was Helen Corke, his Croydon friend. But none of them much resembled what he felt he needed, and ultimately found in his wife Frieda. It may be, however, that we make too much of this; his mother may have prevented a permanent relationship, but Lawrence was sexually neither inert nor ignorant. (He had an affair with a 'progressive' married woman.) The remarkable scene in *The Rainbow* between Will Brangwen and the girl he picks up at the music hall could not have been written by a man who lacked familiarity with this kind of sexual adventure; and we shall need to remember, in speaking of the sexual aspect of his 'metaphysic', that his most extreme speculation had a substructure of experience.

Lawrence's earliest surviving writings of any substance are a handful of poems, the play called *A Collier's Friday Night*, some stories, including an early version of 'The Odour of Chrysanthemums', and his first novel, *The White Peacock*. This last was begun in 1906 and, after multiple revisions, finished in 1910. He needed to finish it, but despised it even before he had done so. Borrowing the plan —to describe the developing relationship between two couples—from George Eliot, the great novelist of his region, he professed no interest in plot, and produced what he called 'a florid prose poem' (*C.L.* 66). The milieu is cultivated middle class; the pits and colliers of the region are almost entirely omitted. This is so understandable, given the youth and the aspirations of the author, that the pretentiousness and falsity of much of the book must be called innocent. As late as *Aaron's Rod* Lawrence was unable to render intellectual chitchat other than clumsily and affectedly. He was still on some ladder leading to refinement, still his mother's son.

For all that, *The White Peacock* is often very impressive, not only in the delicacies of natural description, but in the quiet presence of themes and images that later grew dynamic. Lettie prefers a vacuously cultivated half-man to the earthy George Saxton; finding no satisfaction in him she seeks it in her children. George marries a sensuous motherly woman, and can say of her : 'Meg never found any pleasure in me as she does in the kids' (III. iv). The vicious circle Lawrence was to try so hard to break—the spoiling of women by men, and their consequent spoiling of their sons, who, etiolated by their mothers, will spoil their wives—is already in his first book. The narrator, Cyril, is a cruel caricature of a refined young Lawrence, who cannot quite bear to think of women as sexual beings. The strong George Saxton declines, like Lawrence's father, into drunkenness.

In the chapter called 'Poem of Friendship' (II. viii) the account of the embrace between the burly George and the slender Cyril ('our love was perfect for a moment, more perfect than any I have known since, either for man or woman') is the first statement of a theme that sounds obstinately in later Lawrence, especially in *Aaron's Rod* and *Women in Love*. Most remarkable of these pre-echoes is the gamekeeper Annable. 'He was a man of one idea;—that all civilization was the painted fungus of rottenness. He hated any sign of culture ... When he thought, he reflected on the decay of mankind—the decline of the human race into folly and weakness and rottenness. "Be a good animal, trust to your animal instinct," was his motto' (II. ii). It is Annable who comments upon the peacock which perches on an old stone angel in the churchyard, and defiles it : 'the miserable brute has dirtied the angel. A woman to the end, I tell you, all vanity and screech and defilement.' So do women defile men, as Annable was defiled in his marriage. Like Mellors a gentleman, dropped out, he is also like Mellors unsentimentally harsh about children; like him, too, he is strongly associated with natural life. He meets his death by a fall of stone in a quarry, crushed as in the novel other natural objects—a chick, a woodpigeon, flowers—are crushed underfoot.

Lawrence wrote the Annable passages late. 'He *has* to be there ... he makes a sort of balance. Otherwise it's too much one thing, too much me,' he told Jessie Chambers.[2] When Cyril enjoys the contact of Sexton's naked body he thinks of Annable; a man who has moved beyond women, and who, however unhappily, maintains himself in isolation, a third force between nature and culture. So it will be with Mellors, the gamekeeper of *Lady Chatterley's Lover*, but Mellors does not die; he is reborn into a new world. Here, at any rate, the young Lawrence is exploring the hidden patterns of his imagination.

The other relationships described in the novel are by no means without interest; as Mr Graham Hough has remarked in his perceptive treatment of the book, one cannot dismiss as simple naïvetés of construction 'attempts at saying or symbolizing something Lawrence knew to be important, whose bearing and relevance he cannot yet see'. Many of these matters achieve expression, in one way or another, later; but it is true that there are one or two things in *The White Peacock* which were never again, after the development of a 'metaphysic', to be handled with such inexplicit delicacy. Mr Hough, indeed, finds in the first novel 'a singularly pure and untrammelled kind of discernment' later abandoned in favour of 'something more turbid and more difficult'. And he wonders, sadly, 'what would have become of Lawrence the novelist if he had not found it necessary also to become a prophet'.[3]

The truth may be, rather, that given Lawrence's temperament and talent there was no going forward, once a somewhat reluctant imitation of the old ways of registering human relationships no longer sufficed, except by using some 'metaphysic' as an heuristic instrument. The insecurities of *The White Peacock*, as much as its certainties—Annable in particular—indicate a talent that will not be content with the minute and sympathetic observation of human behaviour; a Rosamond Vincey will never be within the field of his interest. The famous letter to Garnett (see p. 28 below) explains why, but so does *The White Peacock* itself; all the fluff, all the fussy notations and distinctions which had seemed to be the business of the novelist, had to be burned away before one was to come fully into contact with the basic myth : man trapped between culture and nature. Annable is the first recognisable Lawrentian character. The rest, uneasy, cultivated, novelistic, would be destroyed by the metaphysic.

Lawrence went to his teaching job in Croydon in October 1908. His work gave him matter for some poems and stories; and he worked up part of a novel by his friend Helen Corke into another novel, *The Trespasser*, which was written in the spring of 1910 and revised early in 1912. It has some interest as an early example of Lawrence's habit of creatively reworking a text, his own or another's; but *The Trespasser* is almost unanimously regarded as the least of his works. It is fashionably Wagnerian; later Wagner moved Lawrence at a deeper level, as in *Women in Love*,[4] but here it is ostentatious, though qualified by irony, since Helena is a neurotic Wagnerite. There are more hints of the future, as when Helena is described as 'belonging to that class of "dreaming women" with whom passion exhausts itself at the mouth' (*T*. iv). This judgment is supported by a familiar generalisation here couched in Ninety-ish prose : 'For centuries a certain type of woman has been rejecting the "animal" in humanity, till now her dreams are abstract, and full of fantasy, and her blood runs in bondage, and her kindness is full of cruelty' (*T*. IV). Siegmund is rejected, as Annable was by his wife, in the pride of manhood. 'I am at my best, at my strongest . . . She ought to be rejoiced at me, but she is not; she rejects me as if I were a baboon under my clothing' (*T*. VI). When she 'meets his passion' she feels herself blasted; and in his passion there is a kind of surrender to a mother-goddess (*T.* XI). Siegmund meets by chance an old musician friend ('a sort of *Doppelganger*', *T.* XIV), who explains the situation : 'The best sort of women —the most interesting—are the worst for us ... By instinct they aim at suppressing the gross and animal in us ... She can't live without us, but she destroys us. These deep, interesting women don't want *us*; they want the flowers of the spirit they can gather from us. We, as natural men, are more or less degrading to them and to their love of us; therefore they destroy the natural man in us—that is, us altogether' (*T.* XIII).

We may think that Lawrence's lovers were simply frustrated by obsolete conventions, difficulties which women no longer put in the way of their suitors. But he would have rejected this easy opinion, being prepared to allow that the cult of castration he euphemistically described had definable historical origins, but not that it was a local difficulty, easily removed. The whole crisis of civilisation, even the war, he came to think, stemmed from it; sexual candour, natural sexual activity and the full marital relationship, would be restored only with great effort, and after an apocalyptic upheaval. In so far as there are early traces of this doctrine in *The Trespasser* the book has its importance. The suicide of Siegmund—his 'trespass', to use a favourite French pun of Lawrence's—lays the death of a natural man at the door of the refined Helena; and there is something about the design of the book—the ease with which sea and moon are used as symbols, the contrived remoteness of the seaside scenes, Helena's sudden vision of her lover not as part of a myth but as a stooped ordinary man—which helps to validate that conclusion. Ford, who thought it 'phallic' and puritanically obsessed by sex, called it 'a rotten work of genius' (*C.L.* 86). The epithet is class-determined; the allusion is to that element of caddishness the upper classes used to find in the young Lawrence (see *N.* I. 137), but the commendation is not wholly excessive.

SONS AND LOVERS

Sons and Lovers, the masterpiece of Lawrence's first phase, was begun in October 1910. In November he ended his engagement to Jessie Chambers, and on 3 December began one with Louie Burrows. His mother died on 10 December. He restarted the novel, then called *Paul Morel*, early in 1911, but set it aside to write *The Trespasser*. Resuming the *Bildungsroman*, he finished it in May 1912, and rewrote it that autumn. Much of importance occurred between these versions. In January 1912 illness forced him to give up teaching; he returned to the Nottingham area and met Frieda Weekley, the German wife of a professor at Nottingham University College. The composition of his autobiographical novel therefore coincided with a period of multiple crises in his life. It was begun before the death of his mother, which is its climax; it was rewritten at the behest of an early lover, Miriam, and then again under the eye of Frieda after their elopement. It would be difficult to think of any other writer who wrote his life into successive texts of his fiction as Lawrence did; he habitually confronted his tale with new experience, and new interpretations of the past. There is in consequence an abundance, even a confusion, of life; one cannot feel that the published version is the last possible rehandling of the tale; and this openness is not the consequence of inefficiency. Flexibility, the power of a story to challenge a reader (including himself) is one of the marks of the novel as Lawrence wanted it to be, liberated from the burden of finality and completeness placed on it by his enemies, the novelists who, in his opinion, mistook structure for life, and novelistic custom for natural law.

Sons and Lovers is probably still the best known of the novels, and it would be wrong to cavil at this, for it is certainly a great achievement. In the first part the brief inset of the courtship of Paul's parents, the father's gaiety, his 'sensuous flame of life' melting the mother's puritanism, has that singleminded veracity of impression which was consistent, in Lawrence, with more abstract intentions. Morel, in his caressing dialect speaks, as Dorothy Van Ghent notes, Lawrence's language of physical tenderness (she adds that the name of Mellors, the gamekeeper of *Lady Chatterley's Lover* who speaks that language also is a virtual anagram of Morel).[5] This is the dark dancing miner whom marriage will reduce, both physically and morally; whose son will be lost to a mother who makes refinement the instrument of her conquest. The placing of the parents and children, as of the ravaged landscape and its colliers, is done with extraordinary narrative tact and energy. Morel, obscurely fighting for a manhood sapped at the root by the absorbing care of the mother, cuts off the one-year-old William's curls and causes his wife the most intense suffering of her life (Lawrence remembered this and used the same narrative theme to a different but related purpose in *St Mawr*, when Mrs Witt cuts the hair of the groom Lewis). Mrs Morel is locked out by an angry husband; under a great moon she buries her face in a lily, and returns to the house smeared with pollen. This scene is so intensely realised—night scents and sounds, grey-white light, fear and cold—that the mind is satisfied without further interpretation, though interpretation, if offered, will be absorbed. Does the lily, a flower which Lawrence admired for its sexual blossoms and mired roots, daub Mrs Morel satirically, or is there sympathy between them? Miriam is later taken to task for trying to identify with or possess the flowers she is admiring. But Mrs Morel is for once identified with the night; when her normal prudence returns she makes her husband let her in, and his punishment for the misdeed is to be further reduced. There are other scenes in which narrative is transcended, caught up into some symbolic mode, without damage to the relation of acts and persons; for example, the moment when the blood of the mother, struck by the husband, drops into the baby Paul's hair. This boy sleeps with his mother, and lovingly cleans the mire off her fine shoes; episodes of everyday life will tell their own story better when the entire narrative context is capable of assuming, at any moment, large symbolic meanings; an understanding of how this worked is what chiefly distinguishes Lawrence as a critic of fiction, especially in his studies of American literature. Thus it is not enough to say that the perversely close relation of Paul with his mother precludes the possibility, at least during her life, of his satisfactorily choosing a sexual partner; Miriam is not merely a rival but also, in some ways a double; the rejection of her for the mother is also a rejection of the mother.

So too with Morel, the detested father; his defeat is not simply Oedipal; it is also the defeat of the dark virility of the pit, of unashamed and easy male grace and strength, beauty with its roots in muck. And all these meanings are in the complexity of the text, its power to suggest meanings other than that vouched for by a narrator apparently half-committed to Paul's own preference for the mother.

It has been argued that the narrative method alters in Part II; that objective omniscience gives way to a subtler mode, in which we can no longer trust the narrator: 'the point of view adopted is that of Paul; but since confusion, self-deception, and desperate self-justification are essential to that point of view, we can never tell ... where the real truth lies' except 'by seeking out the portrait of Miriam that lies beneath the over-painted commentary of the Paul-narrator.'[6] This nonce-technique Louis L. Martz regards as having served on one occasion only; but Lawrence is the great over-painter, his habitual method is to confront the text again and again, to rehandle it in precisely this style. The product grows progressively more complex in relation to the intention; that is why he insists that we do not isolate an intention and trust it. Trust the tale. If there is more than one Miriam under its surface paint, then so be it. In fact any novel, by virtue of its length, the intermittency of such controls as 'point of view', and the indeterminate nature of narrative, permits a great many such doublings, and consequently an indefinite range of interpretation. And Lawrence, with his fierce confidence in the novel as the *best* way of understanding reality, is not merely permissive; at his best he encourages the fiction to take away the power of meaning from its author. Rewriting, or 'overpainting', was his usual way of achieving this. So there is nothing unusual about his employment of the method in *Sons and Lovers*, though Martz is right to find it there, and his demonstration of its effect on the representation of Miriam is finely achieved.

Jessie Chambers did not like the Miriam she saw—unwilling to let go, subtly wrong in her attitude to the non-human or the animal, too much, in the end, the woman who buttons up or reduces men. She saw how much the confusions of Paul had coloured her image, how unfair his condemnation and rejection of her for a failure in which she shared at least equally. Yet all this is in the book; it is he who, possessed, resents her possessiveness, he whose 'sex desire was a sort of detached thing that did not belong to a woman' (X). The only woman who might really please him would be one he did not know (compare the story 'Love Among the Haystacks', probably written in 1911). And it is he who forces the girl to accept him sexually : 'He said that possession was a great moment in life' (XI). This is what Lawrence later came to call sex in the head. When Miriam makes her sacrifice he identifies the initiatory experience with death. Miriam has two faces, the vital and sensitive, often snubbed by Paul, and the timid, restrained and possessive, both of which somewhat resemble Mrs Morel. Both are visible, simultaneously.

So with Clara : the success with which Lawrence renders the pleasures of this sexual relationship is not always recognised. It is true that she is a licensed mother-substitute;

the first thing Paul does after making love to her is to clean her boots. But the very completeness of his sexual satisfaction sets it apart from life; she is for night, not day. Dawes, so often called a reflection of Morel, is Clara's true husband; Paul ritually fights him and comes to terms with the married couple, as he might with his reconciled parents, but the death that inhabits his sex manifests itself in the same chapter as the fight, when his mother confesses her cancer.

Such are the complexities which life, and reflection upon it, brought into the overpainting of *Sons and Lovers*. The cutting of all the knots is the death of the mother, in the chapter called 'Release'. Paul says goodbye to her, and to Clara; he oscillates between death and a mechanical kind of life, swings back briefly and for the last time to Miriam, and then departs for the future, 'a nothingness and yet not nothing' (XV), walking towards light not darkness. The novel originates in an intense and prolonged personal crisis; it is remarkable that it should be so unselfish, so unsentimental. One could hardly ask for further proof of the seriousness with which Lawrence believed that 'the novel, properly handled, can reveal the most secret places of life',[7] as no other discourse can, and do so beyond the intention, and despite the defences, of its author.

Much has been said of the relation of *Sons and Lovers* to Freud; its theme is Oedipal, and in the later stages of composition Lawrence had learned something about Freud from Frieda—his first contact with a thinker he was repeatedly to attack. The degree to which the personal relationships in the novel comply with Freud's account of mother-fixation is surely a tribute to the accuracy of Freud's generalisation rather than a proof of Lawrence's indebtedness. Freud observed and generalised, Lawrence observed, but believed that the text of a novel was more than an occasion for drawing abstract conclusions. Freud was, as it happens, the kind of scientist Lawrence believed to be incapacitated, by the very nature of his interests and methods, from giving a truthful version of reality. It is nevertheless true, as Simon O. Lesser has remarked,[8] that there are interesting common elements in *Sons and Lovers* and Freud's important, and almost contemporaneous paper, 'The Most Prevalent Form of Degradation in Erotic Life' (1912). This is the disorder Freud calls 'psychical impotence'—impotence which has no physical cause, and is manifested only in relation to some women. There is a conflict between affection and sex, traceable to an incestuous fixation on mother or sister. It may not take the extreme form of impotence, and indeed in most people it does not; but Freud is clear that 'very few people of culture' can achieve an ideal fusion of tenderness and sensuality, and this manifests itself in a lack of sexual desire for women who inspire affection, and is remedied 'in the presence of a lower type of sexual object'. The consequence is an inability to get on with one's well-brought-up wife. And he believes that 'whoever is to be free and happy in love must overcome his deference for women and come to terms with the idea of incest with mother or sister'. Honest men admit the sex act to be degrading; honest women are obliged by the culture to make it secret, and of course the trouble of the men rubs off on them also. The sexual difficulties of the age, Freud was sure, stemmed from the basic Oedipal situation, assisted by another unchangeable condition, the proximity of the genital and excrementory organs in an animal which, since it learnt to walk upright, has tried culturally to sever the associations between them. It cannot be done; the genitals remain animal, and so does love, which perhaps will never 'be reconciled with the demands of culture'.

This diagnosis is certainly directed towards a situation of which Lawrence was aware, though for him 'the demands of culture' originated in and were insisted upon by woman. Paul is almost aware—as is Morel—that his relationship with his mother is not entirely a matter of sexless 'affection'—he is at times a phantom husband. And he knows, however obscurely, that one reason why Miriam will not do is that he attributes to her a denial of animal nature which he associates with superior women—with Clara he has much better sex because she is, in a measure, inferior. The story makes it plain enough that an explanation similar to Freud's is also lurking in it.

Lawrence's own reaction to the sex-culture dilemma proposed by Freud would certainly have been, 'To hell with culture'. And this meant, partly, to hell with women, its agents. Later he was explicitly to reject the Oedipal hypothesis, though he defended with increasing ferocity the position that women inhibited the full expression of a man's inmost self, defiled his angel. His reflections on the genital-excrementatory syndrome persisted through many years, and in practice his answer was to teach the woman better by enforcing it on her in its animal reality. Yet it is clear enough that Freud and Lawrence, however different their instruments and diagnoses, were in a sense talking about the same thing, an epochal sickness with deep roots in the past, and, as to its symptoms as well as its causes, a malfunction of sexual relationships within the culture. Philip Rieff calls them both 'honest heresiarchs', who tried to show us that we were sick from our ideals, and succeeded anyway in demonstrating that we were sick *of* them.[9] Their intellectual traditions were very different, and Lawrence's opinions, mystical and rational, have their origin in English radical thought, not in the clinics of Vienna; but their concurrence, as far as it goes, is testimony that, as Europe moved into the Great War, to speak well of the obvious ills of civilisation one had to reflect deeply on sons and what they love.

Lawrence was soon to feel a need to give systematic form to such reflections; the war developed them and made them urgent, but they are implicit in *Sons and Lovers* and in the poems of *Look! We Have Come Through* which celebrate recovery and marriage. *Sons and Lovers* is the only major work of Lawrence which had no doctrinal double, in which there is no possible dissension between life and what he called 'metaphysic'. Henceforth all is different.

Chapter One   1913–1917

[*The Rainbow, Women in Love*]

I. 'ART AND METAPHYSIC'

'I shall change the world for the next thousand years', said Lawrence to Frieda (*N. I.* 162). Change certainly set in, and Lawrence had something to do with it, although it was another millennialist who actually instituted a thousand-year Reich. There are resemblances—so much may be said without risking association with the most extreme allegations of Lawrence's 'fascism'—between the authors of *Mein Kampf* and *Aaron's Rod* : each of them produced doctrines, recommendations for changing the structure of society and the quality of life, which had to be tried in the fires of action. But one made war and slaughter-camps, the other novels; and one bent the world to the doctrine, the other the doctrine to the world. The latter method produces the more subtle alterations in the quality of our lives.

The relation of doctrine to tale—and he was extraordinarily productive of both—was always, for Lawrence, a difficult and important question. Willie Hopkin asked him during his Croydon period, when he had already written *The White Peacock* and perhaps some of *Sons and Lovers*, whether he 'intended us to read his books as novels or as treatises on the experience of spiritual and bodily aware-ness ... He replied rather casually that if we read them simply as stories we should not get much satisfaction from them. Said he, "When will you discover that what you call the intelligence is a something that cheats you and juggles you all the time. It can make you believe you are right when you are hopelessly wrong—you must have physical vision" ' (*N. I.* 74). Some years later when he was struggling to get *The Rainbow* right, and working on his doctrinal *Study of Thomas Hardy*, he called the struggle between

25

doctrine and tale the 'antinomy between Law and Love'.

'Every work of art adheres to some system of morality. But if it be really a work of art, it must contain the essential criticism on the morality to which it adheres ... The degree to which the system of morality, or the metaphysic, is submitted to criticism within the work of art makes the lasting value and satisfaction of that work ... If Aeschylus has a metaphysic to his art, this metaphysic is that Love and Law are two, eternally in conflict, and eternally being reconciled ... The adherence to a metaphysic does not necessarily give artistic form. Artistic form is a revelation of the two principles of Love and the Law in a state of conflict and yet reconciled ... It is the conjunction of the two which makes form. And since the two must always meet under fresh conditions, form must always be different. Each work of art has its own form, which has no relation to any other form. When a young painter studies an old master, he studies, not the form, that is an abstraction which does not exist ... he studies chiefly to understand how the old great artist suffered in himself the conflict of Love and Law, and brought them to a reconciliation ... It is the novelists and dramatists who have the hardest task in reconciling their metaphysic, their theory of being and knowing, with their living sense of being. Because a novel is a microcosm, and because man in viewing the universe must view it in the light of a theory, therefore every novel must have the background or the structural skeleton of some theory of being, some metaphysic. But the metaphysic must always subserve the artistic purpose beyond the artist's conscious aim. Otherwise the novel becomes a treatise ...' (P.I. 476–9). Later these observations on his own problems as a novelist are transcended by a comprehensive apocalyptic account of the world, to which, however, they are always germane.

During the rest of his life Lawrence worked out and altered his metaphysic, his version of Law, in books that he did not call works of art, and, in his fictions, brought it into conflict with Love. Perfectly reconciled, they would produce what he called the Holy Ghost, the Comforter. Thus a novel might resemble a Lawrentian marriage, and the resemblance is not fortuitous, since they are both types of the living universe. 'The novel is the one bright book of life,' he says; 'Turn truly, honourably to the novel, and see wherein you are man alive ... at its best the novel, and the novel supremely, can help you. It can help you not to be a dead man in life' (*P.I.* 535–8). Lawrence never gave this up; his last novel, *Lady Chatterley's Lover*, repeats the claim even more emphatically. And somewhere in the midst of this flowing text of life there dwells, transformed, the metaphysic. When he read other novelists—Hardy, Tolstoi, Hawthorne—Lawrence was always alert to the distinction between the truth of art and the truth of doctrine; so that he did not hesitate to 'trust the tale' rather than the author, who might well, like Hawthorne, be deceived by his own metaphysical intentions.

The following pages concern themselves largely with the problem of reconciling doctrine and tale as Lawrence faced it in his own mature writing. He was an ideologue as well as an artist. We are often told that we should attend to the major novels as art, and not as repositories of doctrine, that they cannot be cracked open like nuts; and this is true. But Lawrence's ideas, variously understood and misunderstood, have been a force in the world; and it has been the novels, not the treatises, that have put them into circulation. Moreover, as the *Hardy* passage quoted above demonstrates, the originality and formal inventiveness of his fiction derives in large measure from the racking and transformation of ideas by living narrative. If the treatises grow more fantastic and schematic, the novels illustrate the point Lawrence himself makes : in each of them art and metaphysic meet 'under fresh conditions', and their conflict and reconciliation are, as he says, the proper subject of study.

There is a passage in the Preface to the *Fantasia of the Unconscious* which is sometimes quoted by critics who seek to deter us from reading the treatises and the fictions together. 'This pseudo-philosophy of mine,'—"polly-analytics" as one of my respected critics might say—is deduced from the novels and poems, not the reverse.' But this statement is qualified in the next paragraph : 'Men live and see according to some gradually developing and gradually withering vision. This vision exists also as a dynamic idea or metaphysics—exists first as such. Then it is unfolded into life and art.'[1] This reflects his own experience. As E. M. Forster said in his obituary of Lawrence, 'one never knows what his own message will evoke in him, and although I cannot believe it, I believe it was the mainspring of his genius' (*N*. I. 274). In each new novel the metaphysic wrestled with life, by which it was mocked, twisted and finally converted into something unforeseen. The struggle is symbolised by Lawrence's own repeated fight with his text, in version after version; the most remarkable of these agons attended the gestation of *The Rainbow* and *Women in Love*. Setting little store by the first try, he grew in confidence as the 'new thing'—the double novel—declared its shape; and by the time he could rally strongly to its defence he was in a position to enunciate, in a letter to Garnett, a whole new theory—not of being but of the novel—which is as radical a departure from the classic conventions as any proposed since; for it rejects 'character', 'development' and so forth as so many shibboleths, customary but not essential attributes of the novel, having no necessary place in it (*C.L.* 281).

In that famous letter Lawrence allows that he has a certain affinity with the Futurists. He was not on the whole sympathetic to, or even very interested in, the avant-garde movements of his time; if we were to try to relate his innovations to those, virtually contemporary, of Hulme in England or Apollinaire in France, we should be struck at once by his apparent isolation, by the way he works things out for himself. The formative years, for example, of André Breton, can be recounted with reference to large and well-documented movements such as Dada and Surrealism; at a deeper level we could find affinities with Lawrence—for example in common apocalyptic and occult preoccupations —but Lawrence is always working alone. His relationship to the history of ideas in his time is so far below the surface that to write it would be to engage in very delicate and also very speculative excavations. And this is true of his political as well as of his psychological and aesthetic positions.

In what follows I have occasionally touched, rather roughly, on these matters. The most difficult is the political. In the war years—the worst, undoubtedly, of his life— Lawrence sometimes behaved in such a way as to make reasonable observers doubt his sanity; and some who knew him then were willing to say later that by temperament, conviction and desire he had the makings of a Fascist. Cecil Gray said so ('He was ... the stuff of which Hitlers are made,') though he adds that Lawrence was not, like Hitler, an artist *manqué* : 'otherwise we might have been saddled with a similar phenomenon here in post-War years as afflicted Russia, Italy and Germany' (*N. I. 431*). Bertrand Russell, who in 1915 had a much deeper quarrel with Lawrence, said later that he 'had developed the whole philosophy of fascism before the politicians had thought of it', and many years later he held the opinion that the Lawrentian 'philosophy of "blood"' was one that 'led straight to Auschwitz' (*N. I. 283–4*).

Although it cannot be denied that in some of his political opinions, and by virtue also of some aspects of his temperament, Lawrence exposed himself to such charges, Russell was unjust. It was much easier then than it is now to confound benign and malignant political solutions of the manifest and dreadful problems of the world of 1914–18; and Fascism grew from roots that could look innocent enough. But, it is more important to note that Russell refers exclusively to Lawrence's intemperate wartime correspondence, and to his doctrinal work, not to his novels. Gray was right; Lawrence's authoritarianism, his cult of blood, discipline, his leadership mystique, were not dangerous, if only because he was an artist *réussi*. It was in the novels that he wrestled with these transcendent systems. The novels do not have a design upon us; their design is upon the unqualified, uninspected dogmas of the treatises and letters, which must be made to submit to life. Why, asks Lawrence, is the novel the highest form of human expression? 'Because it is so incapable of the absolute ... in a novel there's always a tom-cat, a black tom-cat that pounces on the white dove of the Word.' The novel is *quick*, and contains 'no didactic absolute ... everything is true in its own relationship, and no further ... a theosophist cannot be a novelist ... A theosophist, or a Christian, or a Holy Roller, may be *contained* in a novelist. But a novelist may not put up a fence' (*P*.II. 418–25). So Lawrence in 1925. The novel, the tale, could not become Fascist without becoming dead.

The novels are not all equally successful, and some have their deadnesses; they also have their intrusive didactic absolutes. Lawrence's theory of the novel is supple enough, profound enough, to justify those who believe him to be the greatest of twentieth-century critics. His greatness as a practitioner lies, partly, in the strength and persistence with which he sought to allow *quickness*—the life of the text— to qualify the absolute truth brought in from outside, in a confrontation of Law and Love. The failures confirm the successes; we can see where they go dead.

We might say that the modernity of this master lies not in the metaphysic but in its transformations. He inherited a disposition to invent and to trust transcendent systems, but understood that the pluralities and ambiguities proper to art will not admit them. The texts of his novels lack that kind of directionality—indications of fidelity towards or dependence upon an external system of being—which gives the classics he rejected their characteristic forms. 'Everything is true in its own relationship, and no further.' It is in the great letter to Garnett, long before *The Rainbow* emerged from the struggle with its didactic absolute, that we hear the first hints of a new novel, purged of those customs which had seemed laws; a kind of novel that is still not fully understood. (Pound said that Lawrence had got the point of the modern before he had, for all his efforts.[2]) 'That which is physic—non-human, in humanity, is more interesting to me than the old-fashioned human element—which causes one to conceive a character in a certain moral scheme and make him consistent. The certain moral scheme is what I object to ... You mustn't look in my novel for the old stable *ego*—of the character. There is another *ego*, according to whose action the individual is unrecognisable...' The whole passage is about a change in the apprehension and representation of *character*; but its implications as to the relation between the novel and society, the novel and the world, are enormous. And not the least of them is that ideas which may change the quality of life must, when entertained in the one bright book of life, themselves be changed.

We need not, then, be surprised, that Lawrence hated to be told that his books were 'formless'; people who said that were talking about 'an abstraction that does not exist'—the Form of the Novel, not an encounter, 'under fresh conditions', of Love and the Law, as we shall later find him formulating it. 'Tell Arnold Bennett,' wrote Lawrence to Pinker, 'that all rules of construction hold good only for novels which are copies of other novels. A book which is not a copy of other books has its own construction' (*C.L.* 399). This belief helps to explain Lawrence's method of writing.

There are novelists who work slowly but with certainty,

so that their first drafts, with minor amendments, can go to the typist or printer. Lawrence was not such a writer. He worked under pressure, producing many drafts, all widely different; and this is as true of his last novel as of his first. Each rewriting involved another struggle with the text: deletions, additions, remodellings, further qualifications of doctrine. There is a kind of creative opportunism in this, or rather a desire to catch the momentary flux of life rather than comply with dictates of 'form'. In 1913 Lawrence reviewed Mann's *Death in Venice*, finding in it the deadness of the Flaubertian doctrine, 'Nothing outside the definite line of the book.' Mann's work has none of the rhythm of a living thing' (*P.I.* 308–13). A book, like a life, may have a direction, even a tentative scenario; but it also has contingency, and this must be swept into its rhythmical movement.

Not only did Lawrence radically alter *Sons and Lovers* after Jessie Chambers's comments on the first draft and accept direction at a later stage from Frieda; he could even write a second version, similarly re-imagined, of other people's books, which is what happened in *The Trespasser* and *The Boy in the Bush*; and some non-fiction—notably *Twilight in Italy* and *Studies in Classic American Literature* —also underwent radical revision. (One needs sometimes to be very careful with evidence drawn from such books as *Twilight*, which has many later doctrinal additions.) These revisions are relivings of the text. If life offered new material during the revision period, it went in. Lawrence had the habit of putting in fairly straight accounts of people and incidents, and they simply had to be made to settle in the book; there are striking instances of this in *Women in Love*. He obviously had great confidence in his power to blend these intrusions into the existing text, though now and again we see the process go wrong; in *Kangaroo*, where his creative drive is at its lowest despite the extraordinary rapidity of its composition, Lawrence depends too heavily on such chance offerings, and in one chapter simply copies out bits from a local newspaper, thus affecting a strange shotgun wedding of metaphysic and *faits divers*.

For the most part, however, he was evidently right to take such risks, which are on the side of life and militate against doctrine, character and 'the definite line'. *The Lost Girl*, which opens in the manner and milieu of Arnold Bennett, ends in an icy Italian countryside which Lawrence could not even have imagined when he started the book, and in other ways generates a unique and quite unforesee-able structure. And even in the great books, where there are so many forces at work to shape the narrative and limit the author's freedom, he will insert some character recently met because he seems likely to be part of the book's quick-ness and its rhythm. Such dangerous methods were perhaps, for Lawrence, mere prudence; a book which has this palimpsest-like construction will acquire an opacity, an unmechanical irregularity of line, unlikely to encourage be-lief in the presence of an untransmuted metaphysic, or in those merely geometric forms which represent life but do not enact it, which fail to give the exact curve of the thing.

II. THE SISTERS

All this is a general prelude to some remarks about meta-physic and narrative in the central novels, *The Rainbow* and *Women in Love*, especially the latter; but another pre-lude is necessary, for to understand those books under the aspect proposed one has to know something about Law-rence's life and thought during the war years. His mother died at the end of 1910; in the autumn of the following year he was seriously ill. During his convalescence he rewrote *The Trespasser*, and by a series of decisions prepared him-self for a new phase of his life: he gave up Louie Burrow, to whom he had become engaged in the last weeks of his mother's life; he saw his Croydon friend Helen Corke for the last time; and in the spring of 1912 he said his farewell to Jessie Chambers. Shortly before this he had met Frieda Weekley; he left England with her on 3 May. The death of a parent often signals mysterious upheaval and change in the personal life, but the totality of Lawrence's break with the past is very striking. He was in his twenty-seventh year, and writing in a new way. *Sons and Lovers*, begun in 1910, was for a second time rewritten and new-made in the autumn of 1912, this time under the eye of Frieda. He worked on the poem-sequence called *Look! We Have Come Through*, began and abandoned a novel based on the life of Burns, wrote *The Widowing of Mrs Holroyd*, a play that came into its own only fifty years later, and by March 1913 had written two hundred pages of what later became *The Lost Girl*, a novel he left behind in Italy and resumed only in 1920. He took this book very seriously ('so new, so really a stratum deeper than anyone else has gone ... quite unlike *Sons and Lovers*, not a bit visualised' (*C.L.* 193), and put it aside only because he needed to do a pot-boiler. This was *The Sisters*, which evolved into *The Rainbow* and *Women in Love*.

These were critical years for Lawrence, and the nature of his engagement with fiction was rapidly changing. In January 1913 he had written—not for publication, as he explained to Garnett (*C.L.* 181)—a Preface to *Sons and Lovers*, so that the earlier book did belatedly acquire a metaphysical twin. What is striking is that he finds in his *Bildungsroman*, for all its 'visualising', a symbolic meaning certainly there, but suggestive of the much larger and more ambitious systematisations of belief that were soon to occupy him. These may therefore be said to have their origin in Lawrence's experience, including the experience of writing *Sons and Lovers*. This first 'metaphysical' an-nouncement is, implicitly, an attack on women for ruining men, but it says a great deal more. The Father, says Lawrence, is the Flesh, the Son the Word; and Adam, the first man, was the first Christ, the Flesh made Word. The Flesh is of the Father, unalterable; but men are of the Word, which withers away. The Son, however, has usurped the Father; the Flesh withdraws from us and we are left with the ruined Word—which is to say, we have exchanged physical for mental consciousness. The Word cannot make us one flesh with a woman, and so we must perish.

For the woman is Flesh, and the Father ought truly to be called the Mother, whose Son is the Word, the Utterer. We know God, the Flesh, in Woman. She is the hive to which the Son-bee returns from his work, his Uttering, to be expelled again into work; in this rhythm of uttering and rejoining the Flesh he finds his joy, his Holy Ghost. But if he does not come and go in the proper rhythm the Woman turns him out and finds another man, or rather takes her son for a lover. However, he cannot be her lover wholly; and since she cannot renew him he wastes away. The failure of Man in the Flesh causes women to ruin their sons with love. 'The old son-lover was Oedipus. The name of the new one is legion. And if the son-lover take a wife, then she is not his wife, she is only his bed . . .' So that his wife in turn will long for sons, 'that she may have her lover in her hour'.[3]

The tone of this curious piece is quasi-biblical; it is an obscure sermon on what for Lawrence was a centrally important, though as yet not fully understood, issue. Its theology is not quite that of Lawrence's later trinitarian exercises, and clarity is sacrificed to evangelical afflatus. The relevance of these pages to *Sons and Lovers*—the relationship between father, mother and son—is clear enough; it is the elevation of this into a general metaphysical theme that is difficult to grasp. The scheme of Father (here converted to Mother) as Law and Flesh, Son as Logos and 'Love' or Charity, and Holy Ghost as Reconciler, came to obsess him, and greatly affected his later fiction. The important idea that the regeneration of the race and the individual must come from the liberation of marriage from the Mother, from the cultural and mental aspirations of 'good' women, from all that makes men slaves of the Word, of the head rather than the blood, is first stated here. And henceforth the fiction of Lawrence is often complicated by apocalyptic theology.

Only a few days before he sent the Preface off to Garnett, Lawrence wrote to his friend Ernest Collings a well-known letter which contains another attack on the Word, a statement of belief in the Flesh : 'My great religion is a belief in the blood, the flesh, as being wiser than the intellect. We can go wrong in our minds. But what our blood feels and believes and says, is always true ... All I want is to answer to my blood, direct, without fribbling intervention of mind, or moral, or what-not.' (*CL.* 180.) He warned Collings that he was 'a great bosher' (a characteristic partial withdrawal of the metaphysic) but he is obviously serious, and he also has a desire to spread the doctrine for the good of others. 'People should begin to take me seriously now. And I do so break my heart over England when I read [H. G. Wells's] *The New Machiavelli*. And I am so sure that only through a readjustment between men and women, and a making free and healthy of this sex, will she get out of her present atrophy. Oh, Lord, and if I don't "subdue my art to a metaphysic", as somebody very beautifully said of Hardy, I do write because I want folk—English folk—to alter, and have more sense.' (*C.L.* 204.) This was the programme of Lawrence's work when, with little notion of what he was taking on, he began *The Sisters*, in March 1913.

It soon changed itself into a study of 'the relation between men and women' (*C.L.* 200) and became difficult work, 'like a novel in a foreign language I don't know very well' (*C.L.* 209). By late May there were two hundred and fifty-six pages showing 'Frieda's God Almightiness in all its glory ... I'll make it into art now' (*C.L.* 208). In September he reported 'a new beginning, a new form' (*C.L.* 223) and called the book 'weird ... but perfectly proper' (*C.L.* 224). He was confident that the change he had known in himself could be brought about more generally : the English would awake from their oppressive dream, chuck out 'the nihilists, the intellectual, the hopeless people—Ibsen, Flaubert, Thomas Hardy ... And now our lungs are full of a new air' (*P.I.* 304). England must learn to let go, as Frieda had taught him to do (*C.L.* 225). But he had told Frieda that if his mother had lived she would never have let him go; and declared that he 'would write a different *Sons and Lovers* now; my mother was wrong ...' (*N.* I. 182). Liberation from the mother, the need to let go and give the body its expression in sexual relationships, the regeneration of England— these were the preoccupations of the early days of *The Sisters*, together with a recognition of the dangers of allowing intellect to dominate art itself and 'subdue it to a metaphysic'. This danger was perhaps increased by his reading at the time—Greek religion (Jane Harrison), 'Egyptian influences' (*C.L.* 250)—all part of that remarkable swerve, as noticeable in Lawrence as in the other masters of modernism—towards a new version of the primitivism and occultism which are important elements of the continuity between romanticism and the modern.

He worked fast; by the end of 1913 *The Wedding Ring*, as he now called it, was half done (*C.L.* 259) and by January 10, 1914 it was 'nearly finished' (*I.H.* 174). At this stage the story seems to have covered the Skrebensky part of *The Rainbow* and, very roughly, the present *Women in Love*. In April he was pleading with Garnett to try to understand the 'new thing' that was 'evolving itself out of me' (*C.L.* 273). By the following month he had finished *The Rainbow*, as he now called it; he gave it to a friend to type, and went to London, where, in July, he married Frieda. Now he planned a little book on Hardy; but Garnett went on disliking the novel, and Methuen rejected it. Then the war began. The

Hardy book was written not out of the calm of the preceding months but 'out of sheer rage ... it will be about anything but Thomas Hardy ... queer stuff—but not bad' (*C.L.* 290). This short book, published only in 1936, is a development of the metaphysic and an answer to the great need Lawrence felt, in the military and cultural crisis of 1914, to protect the race from 'the ghastliness and mechanical, obsolete, hideous stupidity of war'. Lawrence represents it as an anti-Freudian attempt to 'get our sex right', to express the need we have of fertilisation 'by the *female*. I don't mean the feminine : I mean the female'. Only the female can 'fertilise the soul of man to vision or being', instil awe instead of pride and assertion, help us 'to realise the tremendous *non-human* quality of life' (*C.L.* 291). The elaboration of these insights into doctrine changed the novelist; we need to ask what the *Hardy* book did to him before he once again took up the rejected *Rainbow*.

III. STUDY OF THOMAS HARDY

Hardy is about possible plenitude of life, symbolised by the poppy : disregarding time, the poppy flares its uniqueness even as it prodigally scatters its seed; it attends to being poppy and the rest follows. This is an example of what we should be, but instead we go in for the wrong kind of self-preservation : the law, the movement for female suffrage which will result only in women making more laws—these are mechanical and life-destroying substitutes for poppy-like self-fulfilment; and their consequence is war. The only good of the war is that it can convince us of the need for a revolution in the heart; it won't matter if many die so long as there is afterwards 'alive in the land, some new sense of what is and what is not, some new courage to let go the securities, and to *be*, to risk ourselves in a forward venture of life, as we are willing to risk ourselves in a rush of death' (*P.I.* 407–8).

Lawrence is again talking about the need to let go, and hinting at the perverted female force of law which prevents the race from doing so, as his mother prevented him. He attacks the cult of work, an expression of that law; work is bad unless it extends human consciousness. The doctrine is evolutionary : with the right kind of human effort—but that must be wholly unmechanical—the ascent of man from undifferentiated tissue to mammals, 'from mammals to man, from man to tribesman, from tribesman to me' (*P.I.* 432) may continue till every man is as distinct an individual as an angel : each man a melody, and, with his neighbours, a harmony. This happiness can come only from the rebirth of the individual; which, according to Lawrence, should occur at twenty or thirty years of age. One is reborn not by taking thought, but by letting go—by a 'fall into the future', or a movement 'to the edge of the unknown' (441).

The means is love. The sexual act is the leap into the unknown; the deposition of seed for continuance of the race is a consequence, not a cause, of this poppy-like fulfilment. 'That she bear children is not a woman's significance. But that she bear herself, that is her supreme and risky fate' (441). So with man; it is not the seed that remains but the expense of the whole spirit that matters. Procreation is the accidental tribute of these momentary immortals to time; the union of male and female, are two distincts which, undivided, generate 'the complete consciousness' (444). Man is hub (did he mean *rim*?) and woman is axle; his motion portrays her motionlessness, and their perfect union is a frictionless union of motion and rest, time and eternity. Lesser unions are unstable, unsatisfying, the man inhibited from his leaping by the insecurity of the woman, the woman unstable because the man cannot be depended upon to convey stability into motion. For 'life consists in the dual form of the Will-to-Motion and the Will-to-Inertia, and everything we see and know and are is the resultant of these two Wills' (447). Perfect duality is 'as yet unthinkable'; thus in races as well as in marriages one Will predominates.

Here, at the point where Lawrence's sexual teaching shades over into racial theory, as it almost invariably does, we may reflect that certain basic insights—on 'letting go', on the polar distinctions and tensions between the sexes, on the rebirth of the self—excited in him the need not only to express them in art, but to develop them into a world-system. The *Hardy* study and its successors soon proceed from sex to more abstract considerations, which are then embodied in very elaborate and systematic structures of thought; the analogy with Yeats's *Vision* is close. Thus the reconciliation of the two Wills, of man and woman, will create a third thing, standing to Law and Love, or Woman and Man, as the Holy Ghost stands to the Father and the Son. This is Lawrence's habitual trinitarianism. The imposition of the idea of separate and contending forces on any situation that will accept it is equally characteristic; we shall see how, in applying it to a diagnosis of the decline and rebirth of cultures, Lawrence is willing to let it generate very extreme opinions.

The *Hardy* study is an important indication of the way in which Lawrence used these principles to explore areas apparently unrelated to his main interests: race, for instance. From the doctrine of Wills emerges the statement that the Jews, being weak in maleness, allowed female inertia to overbear them, and so led in the rush to degeneracy. Monotheism, the Law, are—as we might guess from the Preface to *Sons and Lovers*—female; 'the great assertion of the Male was the New Testament' (452). The New Testament contains the command to be born again, into distinct identity: love and multiplicity invade law and the Jewish monism. The Father and the Son are reconciled by the Comforter. Europe followed the Male Christ; for a moment of perfection at the Renaissance (once again we think of Yeats and the Unity of Being) Male and Female were perfectly fused, and Botticelli signals that fusion. But usually there is more of one than the other. Lawrence seeks the fulfilment of the Law in Love, the flesh in the spirit; but 'since the Renaissance, disappointed in the flesh, the northern races have sought the consummation through Love; and they have denied the Father' (468). It is time the Flesh of the Law and the Spirit of Love were again united.

Such is the mixture of art-history, heterodox trinitarian theology and literary criticism, that Lawrence produces in *Thomas Hardy*. It is only a beginning; for the notions of the surrender of male to female in individuals, and in races; of a dissociation between flesh and spirit since the Renaissance; and of the radical modern error of using love for functional purposes, not for the leap into the unknown, have many further implications. Lawrence found in Hardy's Sue Bridehead an image of the 'ghastly sickness of dissolution', and in her husband Phillotson another, of that excremental death flow which horrifies us because of its proximity to the flow of generation; and these also reflect a phase of cultural history as well as personal disaster. This is not an age when the Consummate Marriage reflects the power of the Holy Spirit to unify Love—the man—with Law—the woman. It is rather that we are at the end of an age of Love, the first having been that of Law; and we shall enter the third only when Male and Female find themselves, unite, and usher in the Holy Ghost. The art of that age is like the Consummate Marriage, knowing 'the struggle between the two conflicting laws and ... the final reconciliation' (515–16). But at present we have only that apocalyptic pause, 'the pause of finality' (513) which is 'not the end'; the end is the reign of the Holy Ghost.

All this Lawrence will develop further, though never with the same optimism. The notion of personal and historical regeneration working in parallel gives rise to a tripartite apocalyptic world-history, which in turn endows the moment of writing—the early war years—with cosmic significance. The decadence of the spirit is almost contemporary with the moment of its regeneration; the new age, the renovation of time, is born out of the death struggles of the old. As with Yeats's historical cones, the tip of one emerging from the base of the other, the moment of transition is a moment of annunciation. In the midst of the Terrors, a sign; after the flood, a rainbow. If this seems an alarming programme for a novelist we may take heart from Lawrence's confidence that 'artistic form is a revelation of the two principles of Law and Love in a state of conflict and yet reconciled...' (477).

IV. THE RAINBOW

It is impossible to know exactly what was in the version of *The Rainbow* which Methuen rejected. Mark Kinkead-Weekes, after a study of the manuscript fragments of *The Sisters*,[4] concluded that the rejected version included material now in *Women in Love*. Wagnerian here as elsewhere, Lawrence had started at the end; he had invented Ursula's affair with Skrebensky to account for her attitude to Birkin, and then continued back to the beginning, as Wagner had to move back from the libretto of *Götterdämmerung*. *The Sisters* was the ur-*Women in Love*; its second version the ur-*Rainbow*, though at first this version went on far enough to include Ursula's meeting with Birkin. *The Wedding Ring* was closer to the present *Rainbow*, though still going on further. *Rainbow i* (the rejected version) contained Ursula's childhood, Templeman (the original of Skrebensky), and schoolteaching, but not Winifred Inger. On November 14, 1914, the *Hardy* being almost finished, Lawrence started *Rainbow ii*. Into it went the experience of writing *Hardy*. Horrified though he was by the war, he evidently saw some good in it—as a gigantic and desperate cultural therapy, as the Terrors that precede a new age. He thought the war would end in 1915, and imagined his novel, finished in March of that year, as appearing at that moment of annunciation. The book came out on 30 September, and Lawrence had to alter his view: 'I'm afraid I set my rainbow in the sky too soon, before, instead of after, the deluge' (*N. I.* 328). In November the book was seized by the police, prosecuted for obscenity and withdrawn by Methuen. For the remainder of the war years Lawrence had little to be optimistic about, in fiction, metaphysic or life.

The Rainbow enacts the ages of Law and Love, and ends at the Pause before the next age (Lawrence probably drafted the blurb, which speaks of Ursula, at the end, 'waiting at the advance post of our time to blaze a path into the future').[5] The first section of the book was almost certainly added to *Rainbow i*, and it is there to give flesh to the concept of the age of Law, of 'blood-consciousness' under female threat. Of course he then reworked the whole; Lawrence was not tacking something on, but modifying the whole structure, and aiming to achieve, in his final pages, that 'Supreme Art' which, as the treatise claims, 'knows the final reconciliation' (*P.I.* 516); the rainbow is the Old Testament type of the epoch-making covenant. At the outset the men sit in a plenitude like that at the beginning of Job, at one with the oneness of the flesh and the world; but the women are beginning to look to them for something else, for something unlike the blood-peace they themselves possess; they want 'another form of life' (*R. I.*) and it seems that what they want is knowledge in their men, and a spiritual apartness, and a new kind of mutual awareness. They want men to be fighting 'on the edge of the unknown'. The meeting with Lydia is enough to move Brangwen in that direction. Their struggles are proper to good marriage; as so often in Lawrence the marriage goes wrong before it goes very right, but it is a good marriage, though proper to its epoch. Neither feels the need to discover and cultivate a difficult regenerate and separate personality for he has no great need of it, and she, the aristocrat, has it already (unlike the Jews who ruined her father). In the next section there is not only a difference of personalities, there is a difference of epochs.

To speak thus of the opening of *The Rainbow* is to leave out all that gives flesh to the word; it is evident to every-body that Lawrence wrote it with an extraordinary devotion to the fullness of experience : the stormy night skies, the corn, the udders of cows, the bodies of men heavy with blood, the brooding eyes of the women—but also the be-haviour of the servant Tilly, and the passionately observed insecurities and certainties of the child—all this has a weight in the hand, a richly laborious craft, that tell us something of the deepest importance about Lawrence, namely the shortness of the passage between life and his art. Again and again he astonishes us with accuracy, with fullness, with the sense of an archaic life. His mind held remotely to the doctrine, intensely to the flow of the text which represented the odd angles, the peripeties, the ec-static memories and climaxes of life. For in the time of *The Rainbow* the power of doctrine was less, and the fertility of textual invention greater. Yet deeply concealed as it is, there can be no doubt that there is a doctrinal skeleton in this first part of *The Rainbow*; and it was in the *Hardy* study that it was articulated. An example of the union of doctrine and 'realist' narrative in this section might be the Swedenborgian proposition about marriage and angels, made by Brangwen at the wedding : it is part of the profuse provision of humorous authentication, yet it also remem-bers the *Hardy* suggestions about spiritual evolution, and the hints at the Consummate Marriage.

We find the same situation, though with a difference, in the part which describes the love and marriage of Anna and Will. We are in a world (we nearly always are in Lawrence) where fathers, apprised of their daughters' intention to marry, ask questions about money, though it is also a world where their deeper resentments are recorded. It is a world where embraces in the stable are of bodies 'keen and wonderful' (IV), touching in each other the centre of reality, yet sharing the world with coughing cows, stirring horses; breathing the sharp ammoniac air. Attention having been deflected, for various reasons, from Lawrence's most remarkable achievements in the rendering of sexual love, we may forget the beautiful accuracy of the opening pages of the chapter called 'Anna Victrix', an account of the intoxication of early married love unmatched in fiction— deeply sensual but shading into the comic, it has a genuine archaic or ritual force—just as the passage concerning Will's attempted seduction of the shopgirl has an exactness and indeed elegance exceeding those of the comparable scenes in *Sons and Lovers.* Even Ursula's violence to her pupil, though related to doctrine, has veracity and fineness. There are moments in Lawrence when one remembers with pleasure that he insisted on his commonness; that he used with profit the knowledge that gave him in his early days an ambiguous reputation among his upper-class acquaintance. When Rachel Annand Taylor said he 'was definitely a cad' (N. I. 137), that he had 'attained some culture the hard way' but still 'there was some slum in him' (N. I. 556) she did not know that she was alluding to the kind of power Lawrence cut off when he was writing *The Trespasser* and admiring Rachel Annand Taylor, but turned on when he was about his serious business later. He had no 'slum' in him, but he knew how men make love to girls in parks and stables, and he learnt that this knowledge was not irrelevant.

Anna and her failed artist husband owe something to Hardy's Sue and Jude as Lawrence discusses them in his *Study*, but there is a profound transformation. Will's reluctance to emerge from voluptuousness into separate male labour has its doctrinal side, but it is also a point at which the doctrine is confirmed by ordinary experience; so too

45

with the pain and conflict of the marriage as it develops, with the deep lapse into voluptuousness after the shopgirl incident and the final defeat of Will by Anna Victrix. It all fits the doctrine, yet it is also the kind of truth novels tell.

The Rainbow possesses a virtuoso range of tones, and the good reader will learn to interpret it with a parallel virtuosity. There are passages which have a kind of narrative singleness in itself highly satisfying—old Brangwen's address to his horse as he sets out for home, drunk in the deluge, or Will's chiding of the little Ursula in his kitchen-garden, are examples of this basic novelistic power. In other places the texture is much thicker. For example, the discussion between Will and Anna about the miracle at Cana : she forcing him out of his comfortable acceptance into an uncomfortable, unwelcome independence of spirit, wanting him at the rim, not at the axle, herself lapsing, victorious, into the stasis of motherhood. The fifty pages of 'Anna Victrix' are in themselves a remarkable demonstration of the use of doctrine to Lawrence as novelist. Will loses; the symbols he carves—his phoenix, his Adam and Eve—are rejected and ruined. In the cathedral—another chapter with a powerful thematic line—we may take Anna's jeering as part of the marital struggle, or as doctrinal; for in the *Study* we learn that the medieval cathedrals are Monist, female tributes to the Law, denials of male separateness—except for the gargoyles; and the arguments about Will's passion for them, and about the sex of the gargoyles, mean much more to Lawrence than the occasion of a family dispute. So with the Lamb and Flag window in the parish church—to Anna 'a silly absurd toy-lamb with a Christmas-tree flag ledged on its paw—and if it wants to mean anything else, it must look different from that' (VI), but to Will a symbol of Christ, of his innocence and sacrifice—of Love, in fact. To Lawrence, steeped in the symbolism of apocalypse, it is even more, being the emblem of the victorious Christ in the last days, and he places it here, ambiguously, in his own first apocalypse. It becomes part of the story of Anna Victrix, which is itself part of the story of the destruction of marriage and society by women denied their passive role by inactive husbands.

Such, then, are the deep harmonies of doctrine and narrative in this text. So flexible has Lawrence become that when we come on a passage of prose that seems to belong not to a novel but a treatise—when the text is subdued by a metaphysic—we can take it in our stride. There is a passage of this kind at the end of Chapter X—an Easter sermon on the Resurrection, occasioned by an account of how the Brangwen children responded to the liturgical year. Precisely because of the mobility of the text this does not strike us as intrusive; Lawrence has learned to accommodate metaphysic by extending rather than restricting the skills of the novelist. The confidence he has already acquired will prevent the reader from introducing the wrong kind of resistance at such points. This is also true of moments when the fiction tentatively explores obscure aspects of the theory, as in the Winifred Inger passages. Lawrence, his fierce separation of male from female established, wondered about the homosexual relations possible on either side of the divide. Himself attracted to men (though severe on sodomy) he speculated also about lesbianism. That he should do so seems well enough in tune. The range of the novel is great, and we have learned to be flexible too.

The third section of *The Rainbow* consists of that part of the double novel which Lawrence introduced in order to prepare Ursula for her later encounter with Birkin. Skrebensky brings to her that admired aristocratic isolation, that maleness she associated with the Sons of God who lay with the daughters of men, and who were not the servile children of Adam. The necessary struggle, the necessary disillusion, that follow, are certainly doctrinal, yet count among the most magnificent of Lawrence's fictional achievements. The climactic scene of lovemaking on the dunes, Ursula

mad, at her crisis, a harpy in the moonlight, is unlike anything in any other novel—easily represented, by those who
will not trust Lawrence, as absurd and overwritten, but
merely at the extreme range of the voice we can learn to
trust, a voice capable of authenticating a hidden world of
feeling and behaviour, of which this is the edge. There can
be no question, presumably, about the two stackyard
scenes. Lawrence probably wrote the second, with Ursula
and Skrebensky, first.

> There he saw, with something like terror, the great new
> stacks of corn glistening and gleaming transfigured, sil-
> very and present under the night-blue sky, throwing
> dark, substantial shadows, but themselves majestic and
> dimly present. She, like glimmering gossamer, seemed to
> burn among them, as they rose like cold fires to the
> silvery-bluish air. All was intangible, a burning of cold,
> glimmering, whitish-steely fires. He was afraid of the
> great moon-conflagration of the cornstacks rising above
> him. His heart grew smaller, it began to fuse like a bead.
> He knew he would die. (XI)

Ursula is seized by 'a sudden lust', a cold, brilliant desire;
again and again the language insists on cold crystalline bril-
liance, the salt destructiveness of all the powers that are
hostile to living sex. A generation earlier Will and Anna
went to the stackyard, lit by a golden moon, and put up
sheaves together.

> The air was all hoary silver ... 'You take this row,' she
> said to the youth, and passing on, she stooped in the next
> row of lying sheaves, grasping her hand in the tresses of
> the oats, lifting the heavy corn in either hand, carrying it,
> as it hung heavily against her, to the cleared space, where
> she set the two sheaves sharply down, bringing them to-
> gether with a faint, keen clash. Her two bulks stood lean-
> ing together. He was coming, walking shadowily with

the gossamer dusk, carrying his two sheaves. She waited
near by. He set his sheaves with a keen, faint clash, next
to her sheaves. They rode unsteadily. He tangled the
tresses of corn. It hissed like a fountain. He looked up
and laughed.

And so on for several unfaltering pages, the moon revealing
Anna, laying bare her bosom, before the clash of mouths
and love-declarations.

Friction is already, in the *Hardy* study, a word for the
evil in a sexual relationship. But in the Anna passage the
hiss and clash of the corn is a kind of organic premonition
of sexual surrender. Her daughter, later to be called, by
Rupert Birkin in his bitterness, a moon-goddess, is about to
engage in an act of destruction, the description of which
was a totally unprecedented task, but one for which Lawrence found the means. His Ursula is no suffragette, but a
woman who finds only death in the old sexual order, a
death reflected in the sight of England grown meagre and
paltry. Lawrence took his greatest risk with the conclusion,
in the prose-poem of Ursula and the horses, in the sickness
which burns out an epoch in her life and England's—or so
he allowed himself, at this time, to hope—thus preparing
for the age of the Reconciler, who will bring the dualities
into life-giving tension. The colliers—always for Lawrence
men of another, darker life—wait in their warped and
stiffened bodies for the great liberation; and over the sad
corrupted landscape glows the premature rainbow. 'She
knew that the sordid people who crept hard-scaled and
separate on the face of the world's corruption were living
still, that the rainbow was arched in their blood and would
quiver to life in their spirit, that they would cast off their
horny covering of disintegration, that new, clean, naked
bodies would issue to a new germination ... She saw in the
rainbow the earth's new architecture ...'

The closing passage has images—of separateness, of

beetle-like carapaces—that will persist in Lawrence as his mind grows darker; but although the doctrine suggested its form it is validated by the power of the fiction itself, by the confidence the text has taught us. F. R. Leavis called it 'oddly desperate', a way of ending one book to get on to another in which there would be no such necessary lapses into the 'wholly unprepared and unsupported'.[6] This is surely wrong; the first version of apocalypse required such a conclusion, and it was well prepared. The book—it is still astonishing to reflect—was called filthy, partly because of the scene in which the pregnant Anna dances before a glass. It is the reaction of a mere consumer; Lawrence's readers must produce. They must also understand by remaking the metaphysic as it exists, not raw, but as part of the tissue of the narrative and the rhetoric, which are not subdued.

V. THE CROWN

Lawrence now decided that the *Hardy* study needed expansion. He was changing; meeting new people, for example Bertrand Russell and Lady Ottoline Morrell; becoming more vehement about his charismatic role, more apocalyptic in his talk. The war, he often said, killed him, and he awaited resurrection (*C.L.* 310); 'being risen from the dead, I know we shall all come through'. Early in 1915 he felt that he had been 'dead as a corpse in its grave clothes' (*C.L.* 314), but now he was 'waking'. *The Rainbow* had rescued him; 'I am coming into my full feather at last'.[7] And the Utopian future seized him; Rananim, his ideal society, could be England, its inhabitants those whom an earlier English apocalyptist had called 'God's Englishmen'. He saw the need for revolution to achieve this (*C.L.* 317, to Russell) but it would be a revolution primarily in the relationship of men and women, a break with an old world of sex, which he thought of as relying on masturbation, or on sex merely as a substitute for it. He also advocated the abolition of private property (*C.L.* 322); and as his programme expanded he entered into his disastrous association with Russell, and decided to rewrite *Hardy*. His object, as he told Lady Ottoline, was simply to procure the regeneration of the race, to 'give a new Humanity its birth' (*C.L.* 325). Russell persuaded him to abandon the Christian terminology of the *Hardy* study; he began the new treatise in March, gave it up, resumed it in April, finished it in May, and rewrote it between June and September. Three of its six chapters were published in Middleton Murry's shortlived review, *The Signature*. The whole thing was eventually included in *Reflections on the Death of a Porcupine* (1925).

The Crown is what the lion and the unicorn are fighting for, but in Lawrence's allegory they represent the stability of two equal and opposite forces, so that neither should win it. The lion is our dark nature, the unicorn our light; the strife and equilibrium is the third of the trinity, reconciling the two eternities between which we exist. The argument is not fundamentally different from that of *Hardy*, but it is more rapt. In a person, or in an epoch, Law or Love may predominate; but perfection lies in their balance of the two opposing tendencies or streams; there is a possible moment, as of eternity, when Beginning and End and all other opposites are reconciled. At the moment of writing they were not: 'For the stiffened, exhausted, inflexible loins of our era are too dry to give us forth in labour, the tree is withered, we are pent in, fastened, and now have turned round, some to the source of darkness, some to the source of light, and gone mad, purely given up to frenzy ... then began chaos, the going asunder' (*P.*II. 371–2).

The Going Asunder is the critical epoch of *Women in Love*. The war is the meaninglessness which persists when the two floods of night and day are asunder, when there is no 'iris between the two floods' (*P.*II. 373). The appearance of the rainbow must be delayed; so must the eternal union of man and woman.

One theme is more positively stressed than before : indeed Lawrence gives it a chapter to itself. This is 'The Flux of Corruption'. In accounting for the degree to which the going asunder had progressed he speaks of the dark returning to the dark after knowing light, as the cabbage, having aspired to flower, grows rotten at the heart. This is our corruption; our effort at flowering goes into corruption instead. We even 'enjoy ... this being threshed rotten inside. This is sensationalism, reduction of the complex tissue back through rottenness to its elements. And this sensationalism, this reduction back, has become our very life, our only form of life at all' (388). Sex is 'frictional reduction', and the same sensationalism is expressed in the war. So potent are the forces of dissolution that our consciousness and civilisation are held together only by a sort of evil rind : 'so circumscribed within the outer nullity, we give ourselves up to the flux of death, to analysis, to introspection, to mechanical war and destruction, to humanitarian absorption in the body politic, the poor, the birth-rate, the mortality of infants ... It is the continued activity of disintegration' (392).

The imagery of corruption now took increasingly hold of Lawrence's mind (he often compared people he disliked to beetles, messes inside carapaces). To assume that the world is merely what is inside the case is modern egoism. But when movement forward to a new epoch seemed blocked, Lawrence entertained the idea that one way to make it possible was to make everything get worse. Looking around him, seeing frictionally reductive sex, the women trying to look like children, the cinema with its phoney heroines (he always thought of the cinema with loathing, as a sort of masturbatory brothel) he concluded that the Holy Ghost, who would lead us into the blossoming time, was missing; the first victim was sex, and true sex had been usurped by a deathwish, as the war showed. Perhaps corruption and destruction must be the way forward. 'In corruption there is divinity ... in the soft and shiny voluptuousness of decay, in the marshy chill heat of reptiles, there is the sign of the Godhead ... decay, corruption, destruction, breaking down is the opposite equivalent of creation' (402). Corruption, then, will 'break down for us the deadened forms' (*P*.II. 403), break the rind. Its emblem is the snake, 'the spirit of the great corruptive principle, the festering cold of the marsh' (407). By sinking deeper into corruption, we may break out of our false universe, and begin again.

This new obsession is a measure of the changed tone of Lawrence's second apocalypse, *Women in Love*. As the war went on he developed it. In 'The Reality of Peace', published in 1917, once again under the sign of the snake in his 'festering marshy border' (*P*.I. 678), he speaks of the serpent and the marsh as 'within me'. The desire for creation and the desire for dissolution balance in the psyche and in the body. 'How shall it be a shame that from my blood exudes the bitter sweat of corruption on the journey back to dissolution; how shall it be a shame that in my consciousness appear the heavy marsh-flowers of the flux of putrescence, which have their natural roots in the slow stream of decomposition that flows for ever down my bowels?' (679). The processes of generation and corruption—of the life- and the death-flow—are now explicitly related to genital and excrementatory functions. Here is the battlefield; here a third force will reconcile them. The obsession grew stronger: Lawrence often returns to this theme, which is of great importance in his finest polemical work, *Pornography and Obscenity* (1929); but the first and most important manifestation of the revised and now darkened metaphysic was to be *Women in Love*—fittingly, since art is still the great image of the Comforters, the reconciler of the two tendencies or streams.

VI. WOMEN IN LOVE

Lawrence took up the most recent draft of what had been the earliest-written part of *The Sisters*, rewrote it between April and October 1916, and revised it many times subsequently. He meditated apocalyptic titles—*Dies Irae* and *The Latter Days*—before settling on the one we have. The book was written in a bitter time, when Lawrence himself was desperate and strident. Mark Kinkead-Weekes finds in the earlier drafts a good deal of raw dogmatising; a character is there specially for the purpose, 'voicing Lawrence's world-hatred and his hopes for Rananim, preaching sermons from unpublished chapters of *The Crown*, and insisting on a new post-*Rainbow* theory of the need for male leadership and female submission'.[8] Characteristically—for he had not lost his sense of the rights of narrative, would not subdue it to a metaphysic, however potent—Lawrence modified all this, so that, as Kinkead-Weekes observes, '*The Crown* will not show us how Lawrence learnt ... to hold the apocalyptic in that odd tension with the colloquial ... that makes *Women in Love* such a startlingly different experience from *The Rainbow*'.[9]

Yet the book *is* an apocalypse. Lawrence said when he finished it in November 1916 that it frightened him, 'it's so end of the world' (*C.L.* 482). He called it 'purely destructive, not like *The Rainbow*, destructive-consummating'. Next summer he said that Europe was having the flood without the rainbow : 'We have chosen our extinction in death, rather than our Consummation' (*C.L.* 519). And he goes on to speak of *Women in Love* as the book of this death-drive.

He had no expectation of the book appearing immediately, and did not even want it to be published in the world it represented. We must not forget Lawrence's almost hysterical distress at this time. The banning of *The Rainbow*, the failures in private relationships—with Murry, Russell,

Lady Ottoline (friends who, with others, appear in disagreeable transmutations in *Women in Love*)—the hopeless dream of Rananim, the struggle with Frieda—all these drove him to violent despair. Proclaiming himself dead, he was absorbed by imagery of resurrection and by what seemed to lie behind conventional Christian theology and symbolism (*C.L.* 300ff); he lusted for the New Life, calling his grave a 'womb' (*C.L.* 330); he would have liked to kill people, but instead compiled programmes for political revolution: 'There must be a body of chosen patricians. There must be women governing equally with men, especially all the inner half of life. The whole must culminate in an absolute *Dictator*, and an equivalent *Dictatrix*' (*C.L.* 354). This bluster, later ridiculed by Russell, reflects genuine social and spiritual uncertainties: the shrewd sense of the younger Lawrence was clouded by circumstance. 1915 was for him the end of the old world; he blustered out of his own insecurity but also because out of a deep sense of crisis. Delavenay, minutely studying these years, says Lawrence passed, between the beginning of the war and the end of 1915, through a great visionary crisis in deepening isolation.[10] He tried to escape to the New World, but only got as far as Cornwall, where he spent two grim and hysterical years, exploding with hatred against friend and enemy alike. The 'Nightmare' chapter of *Kangaroo* is the best guide to Lawrence's feelings in these years.

It is hardly surprising, therefore, that the 'metaphysic' should have acquired an interest in corruption, and a new stridency to express it. Yet although to collaborate with corruption now seemed a kind of epochal necessity, there was still utopian hope in Lawrence's mind. Out of this stasis, this evil Pause, might come the true reconciliation of all the opposites, light-darkness, creation-corruption, man-woman. Modern sex may for a while recoil with the death-flow, *pour mieux sauter*.

About the time he was writing *Women in Love* Lawrence

revised some earlier Italian travel pieces, which were published in 1916 as *Twilight in Italy*. The revision incor-
porates much metaphysic, and the book reflects some of the
preoccupations of *Women in Love*. There is, for example,
an elaboration of the distinction between blood- and mind-
consciousness, the establishment of the will to separateness
in the lumbar ganglia, the Holy Ghost presiding over the
union of opposites. Ours is the point of ultimate strain, but
the crisis is already evident in *Hamlet* : 'a sense of corruption in the flesh makes Hamlet frenzied ... The whole
drama is the tragedy of the convulsed reaction of the mind
from the flesh, of the spirit from the self, the reaction from
the great aristocratic to the great democratic principle.'[11]
Walking in a lemon garden or thinking about a fat Italian
Hamlet, Lawrence still extended and deepened his trinitarian version of the world crisis : psychological, political,
literary, art-historical, it all came down to the sexual dualities still : man-woman, sex-excrement; the Comforter to
reconcile.

These ideas of Lawrence's are shaped by his own life and
mind, but they conform to type. Apocalyptic notions common to all who feel that upon them the ends of the earth
have come, do tend so to conform. The medieval prophet
formed his elect group and set out for the city of God, at
the same time urging new modes of sexual conduct on his
flock.[12] His guidebook was the Book of Revelation, as it
was Lawrence's, from his youth to his last book, called
Apocalypse. All his important novels are in a sense allusions
to Revelation. The crisis of one's times, and the rules for
conduct in it, are properly sought there.

The Joachite interpretation of history, a thirteenth-cen-
tury triadic division founded on Revelation, has proved
very persistent. Most familiar to us, probably, from Blake's
Everlasting Gospel, it tends to appear at revolutionary and
chiliastic epochs (such as the mid-seventeenth century in
England); later it was part of the mystical basis of Nazi

thought; the Third or thousand-year Reich is Joachim's epoch of the Holy Ghost, to be preceded by the Joachite Pause, the transition between epochs, between the violent decadence of one phase and the renovation brought by its successor. Lawrence followed this pattern, taking 'the pulse of finality' (*P. I.*), gathering his elect, dealing ruthlessly with the rest. His historical triad makes him what Kant called a 'moral terrorist'[13] and the war provided his terrors. The Joachite pattern had its adherents in the self-conscious Decadence of the late nineteenth-century, a period in which many also exhibited an interest in occultism similar to Lawrence's. In Dostoievsky, particularly, but also in Mann, he found evidence that civilisation was swirling away with the stream of corruption, in what he came to see as a necessary dissolution.

Parallel speculations, more or less extravagantly expressed, abound in the writing of the time. Reading Lawrence on the Renaissance, or on the Civil War, one is reminded strongly of his contemporaries Worringer and Hulme, whom he had not read; Eliot's 'dissociation of sensibility' is only a more cautious and more literary version of a doctrine to which Lawrence gave a cosmic sweep, and both saw the work of art as the temporary representative of the Reconciler who ended that dissociation. Lawrence was reading the Cambridge anthropology so important to Eliot, and also works on occult symbolism—all contributed to his system-building. He may, it has been suggested, have developed some of the racialist extensions of his theory from Houston Chamberlain, whose *Foundations of the XIXth Century* (published in 1899, translated 1910) had many admirers in England, and was to be an important source of Nazi thought.

Chamberlain was a renegade Englishman, a son-in-law of Wagner, whose biography he wrote. He was learned, crazy, and a leading propagandist of the German cause during the First World War. For him the nineteenth was the great century of transition: 'it dangles between empiricism and spiritism, between *liberalismus vulgaris*, as it has been wittily called, and the impotent effects of senile conservatism, between autocracy and anarchism, doctrines of infallibility and the most stupid materialism, worship of the Jew and Anti-Semitism . . .'[14] For Chamberlain the central event of history was the awakening of the Teutons in 1200. Eventually they achieved the Italian Renaissance (purely Teutonic) and everything else: 'Our whole civilisation today is the work of one definite race of men, the Teutonic'—which included genuine Celts and Slavs. At 1800 a turning point was reached; the Jews grew powerful, and were to culture (founded on Teutonic Christianity) as the phylloxera beetle to the vine; though that also led to the cultivation of a new vine. He had nothing against the Jews except that they belonged to an old world and an old religion, and were not Teutonic. The one pure, manysided race must take over and bring the *Völkerchaos* (the chaos of peoples) to an end; the Teutons must be as careful of racial purity as the Jews, whose religion was 'a direct criminal attempt upon all the peoples of the earth', since it promises that the Jews will 'inherit the land for ever' (Isa. 60. 21).[15]

If this writer was, as Paul Delavenay has claimed, an important source, one should nevertheless note some sharp differences between his position and Lawrence's. They share a Joachite pattern, certainly. They each have a doctrine of blood- and race-consciousness, and thought of Jews as female, monotheist, law-orientated. But to Lawrence it is the notion that the Jew has progressed farther than the Nordic races to corruption that counts, and this progression does not interest Chamberlain. Delavenay even suggests that there was in the *Rainbow* prosecution a secret political motive, namely a supposed connection between Lawrence and Chamberlain; as a major propagandist the latter often commented, as Russell and Lawrence did, on the venality of British war aims.[16]

But the truth is that racism, especially anti-Semitism, were part of the climate of these years, and so were doctrines of 'blood-consciousness'. In that seedbed of modern ideologies grew not only fascism, but other less malignant doctrines we would no longer associate with it. For example, Delavenay also argues that the source of Lawrence's views on the sexual arrangements of his millennialist colony derive from the American commune-leader Noyes.[17] This interesting man founded the community at Oneida, argued for polygamy (as Lawrence occasionally did, in letters but notably in *The Boy in the Bush*) and for the dissociation of the pleasures of sex from its procreative function, as Lawrence did as early as *Hardy*. Noyes remarked that God, in Genesis, puts pleasure before procreation; the sexual relation, he thought, reflected that of Father and Son. When forced by the law to abandon 'complex' marriage, he paired off his men and women at random. Lawrence would not have done this; and there is no mention in his writings, as far as I know, of the practice called *coitus reservatus*, for which the Oneida community was famous. Lawrence does have Noyes-like moments.[18] But the truth is again that no source is necessary; with his own variations, Lawrence is conforming to a prophetic typology.

One more name here needs consideration: Edward Carpenter. Best known as a disciple and imitator of Whitman, he was also a propagandist for homosexuals; he became a sort of Yorkshire sage without losing his connexion with the London socialist avant-garde. Shaw admired him; Forster has recently explained how a visit to Carpenter stimulated him to write *Maurice*. He was a friend of Lawrence's Eastwood friends, and Lawrence, who could have been in touch, during his Eastwood days, with many important people on the left, might easily have met him. He doesn't so much as mention Carpenter; but it does seem likely that he knew some of the books, such as *Love's Com-*

ing of Age (1895), *Civilisation, its Cause and Cure* (1889) and *The Intermediate Sex* (1908).

Carpenter, once famous, is half-forgotten. He was the first modern English writer on sex, and regarded sexual reform as a precondition of the improvement of society at large. His socialism was of the English type, developed from an older non-conformity grown more secular, eclectic and cultured. This is Lawrence's milieu also. Within it men and women might, without affectation, discuss Nietzsche, Marx, Darwin and Hindu religion. Carpenter concerned himself with theosophy and yoga, as Lawrence did later; and like Lawrence he had inclusive theories of history. But although there could, perhaps must, have been contact, the important thing is that Lawrence, when he sounds most his own prophetic self on these subjects, or on education or homosexuality, is more in the tradition of an English socialist mysticism than we might now suppose. A future Prime Minister—Ramsay Macdonald—was the secretary of the Fellowship of the New Life, a commune which studied Swedenborg, Carpenterian topics, and much else. In it one could detect the seeds of apparently very different growths, from English Socialism to several varieties of Fascism, including National Socialism.

Carpenter spoke of the desirability of a non-intellectual 'blood-knowledge', anticipating Lawrence, for example, in the letter of December 8, 1915 to Bertrand Russell, which affirms, not for the first time, a belief in a blood-consciousness which must not be tyrannised by 'mental consciousness', and which is capable of absorbing knowledge without the intervention of the mind. Carpenter's thinking on race tempted him into anti-semitism. Furthermore, he sought a Reconciliation between the sexes; and he had some notions about the necessity for male leadership.

In all these matters Lawrence bears him a certain resemblance. A blend of theosophy, socialism, sexual reformism, evolutionism, religious primitivism, was common enough in the avant-garde thinking of the time, a time when there was unanimity among intellectuals on at least the need for change. Politics mixed easily with spiritualism, secret society lore, a revised Christianity, Wagnerism, Ibsenism (Shaw recommended all Fabians to read Carpenter, and admired at least the title of *Civilisation, Its Cause and Cure*). Nietzsche was newly available in cheap translation. Out of this kind of situation comes not only fascism, but *The Plumed Serpent*; not only Auschwitz but garden cities and communes, not only votes for women but new theories of history and of the psyche. The family is large, and may be said to include, in remote degrees of kinship, Jehovah's Witnesses, Reichian therapy and the late poetry of Yeats. A writer might be induced to dream of an aristocracy or a dictatorship—many besides Lawrence did; one might revere absolute authority even as one flouted it. Lawrence certainly did persuade himself to hold some detestable beliefs; the metaphysic steered him into speculations about male supremacy, and the leader-principle, about the necessary subordination of the black and Jewish races and hatred for the underdog. These were not, except in the peculiar form of their systematic expression, unusual views for the time. Beneath them all is the strong period sense of historical dissolution, the need for renovation.

But for all the excesses into which he was swept, Lawrence remained an artist. The powerful vein of scepticism is a highly important, indeed essential part of his equipment as a writer. As he said in *Hardy*, the metaphysic that gets into a work of art must be criticised there. He took good care that it was so criticised in *Women in Love*; scepticism hovers like the Reconciler himself over the junctures of narrative and doctrine. And as he rewrote, struggling again and again with the narrative, Lawrence put his thumb in the scale, over and over again, not for the doctrine, but for the sceptical appraisal of it that would prevent its taking the whole thing over. The novel, if it's alive, 'won't let you tell didactic lies ... You can't fool the novel' (*P*. II. 417).

Women in Love was furnished with a prologue (*P*. II. 92–108) which Lawrence suppressed. It tells of a homosexual attraction between Crich and Birkin, which in the novel he sublimed; and it also speaks of Birkin's love relation with Hermione. This is fairly straight *Crown* material; the relationship is 'frictional', going with the flux of corruption : 'they penetrated further and further into the regions of death, and soon the connexion with life would be broken'. Birkin, an educational theorist, is concerned about the role of education in a world that is in the same stage of the process as he and Hermione, where no knowledge will serve save that of 'unanimity of disintegration' and a cherishing of the unknown future 'when the season of death has passed away'. His problem is to 'get away from this process of reduction', to find something to hold on to in this epoch of decomposition. He seeks it in other women but grows 'gnawed, bitter and a little mad', still knowing, however, that he must not separate himself wholly from the possibility of experiencing true desire, which would involve the body as well as the spirit and the head, where reside the experiences with Hermione. This is metaphysic; only the need of a relationship with a man to complete that with a woman is unfamiliar from *Hardy*, and this was something Lawrence was trying to find out about not only in life, with Middleton Murry, but in the changing text of his new novel. But the real importance of the Prologue is precisely that Lawrence struck it out. As the narrative and the metaphysic were forced into reconciliation this schematic opening was purged; the relationship between the men becomes what it is in the book, a much more problematical thing; and the perverse excesses of Birkin's relationship with Hermione are merely recalled in relation to the critical passages on sexual creativeness and dissolution—the two in tension—within the narrative itself.

Women in Love is a unique masterpiece, but surely those who, in their day, failed to see this were forgiveable. What we have taught ourselves to read as complexity presented itself as opinionated confusion; what seems audacious looked absurd. Thus a by no means imperceptive contemporary reviewer called Lawrence's muse 'aesthetically unchaste'—'His genius has consorted with life and has acquired mystical imperfections, nail-prints in the palms'; and another found that 'some shocks make you giggle', especially 'in a novel where all the characters suffer the pangs of dissolution several times a week'. Middleton Murry's review, though hostile, was the first critique of the book to see its destructiveness: 'Mr Lawrence's consummation is a degradation, his passing beyond a passing beneath, his triumph a catastrophe.'[20] Murry, who hated the book, understood it better than most; later he spoke of Lawrence as one of the few writers who 'struggled with the spiritual catastrophe of the war in the depths of their souls ... they regard the war as a climacteric event, not only in their own subjective experience, but also in the spiritual history of the world. For them it marked the end of an epoch of the human consciousness.'[21] Hence the attempt, in *Women in Love*, to take us through a hideous but necessary process of dissolution. Lawrence, he assures us, bore him no grudge: 'I had taken it seriously, and nobody else had done that.'[22]

The metaphysic must indeed be taken seriously, but not simply extracted. 'In his queer make-up', said Forster in his obituary, 'things were connected, and ... if he did not preach and prophesy he could not see and feel ... You cannot say, "Let us drop his theories and enjoy his art", because the two are one.'[23] Just as *Hardy* helped Lawrence to see the shape of *The Rainbow*—though that novel is by no means a simple vehicle for the *Hardy* ideas—so *Women in Love* needed its proper metaphysic. It is not a novel of extended arcs, like its predecessor; it proceeds by awful discontinuous leaps; its progress enacts those desperate religious plunges into an unknown Lawrence so much wanted. Yet, like a great many others who have made or wanted to make such leaps, Lawrence was not deficient in commonsense, even in intellectual and spiritual prudence. This is something one feels often in the poems, in his sudden ironies, in what Richard Hoggart calls his 'nicely bloody-minded' tone: 'We trust the visionary more because it's rooted in the solid and down-to-earth.'[24] One of the achievements of the novel is to criticise the metaphysic, both by attacking Birkin and by obscuring doctrine with narrative symbolisms capable in their nature of more general and more doubtful interpretation. Just as Ursula and Gudrun were originally Frieda, though differentiated and transformed over the years, so Birkin was the voice of the hectoring preacher Lawrence, and is yet reviled, justly ridiculed, and in the end prevented by the narrative both from being right and from being able to say he has come through.

We begin with the individual spirit, the race and the world at the end of their tethers; yet we also begin with two intelligent provincial girls talking, at about the same level of seriousness as the sisters at the beginning of *Middlemarch*, about marriage—not wanting it, confused about it, but by no means in distress. They walk into the colliery landscape, chthonic, *post-mortem*, a landscape of ghouls, hideous but with a strange inhuman vitality. The machine has turned England and its people into this kind of underworld: the English have led the rush into dissolution. Before the first chapter is over we have seen Gudrun choose Gerald, master of the ghouls, his icy beauty representing a Nordic depth of corruption; and we have seen Hermione as an image of the passional life corruptly led in the mind, and rejected by Birkin as he struggles against this corruption. The words 'dissolution' and 'corruption' haunt the book, and are closely associated with Hermione.

Though every major section in the novel is a new leap, Lawrence established certain recurrences of language and image which ensure continuous narrative and doctrinal pressure; so that although we think of sections of the book—'Moony', 'Water-Party', 'Rabbit'—as having an un-usual distinctness, we also remember it as a whole. To take one instance, the theme of Gerald's guilt. Much of the time Gerald is a plausibly sensible, amused figure; but at the out-set we are reminded that he killed his brother, not because he thought, like Birkin, that 'people don't really matter', but in an accident. Birkin ponders this. 'Is there no such thing as pure accident? Has everything that happens a uni-versal significance? ... He did not believe that there was any such thing as accident. It all hung together, in the deepest sense' (II). What he means is that the text of life is like that of a novel; that on some possible reading it all hangs together, every incident referable to some continuing encodement.[25] Two chapters later Gudrun and Ursula revert to the topic. Gudrun finds such accidents more terrifying than murder, because murder is willed. 'Perhaps there *was* an unconscious will behind it,' says Ursula. They disagree, Gudrun savouring the terror of the meaningless. We are reminded of this earlier accident of Gerald's immediately before the accidental death of his sister, in 'Water-Party'; he has declared his love for Gudrun, but walks beside her, 'set apart, like Cain'. Birkin and Ursula are discussing corrup-tion, the 'dark river of dissolution'. The passage is pure doc-trine ('we find ourselves part of the inverse process, the blood of destructive creation'—with which Gudrun and Gerald are specifically associated), and the associated imagery of marsh, serpent, swan and lily is all there. Birkin will not quite agree that we are *all* 'flowers of dissolution—*fleurs du mal*', at this end of the world, but he comes near to saying so, and Ursula is angry, chiding him as so often : 'You only want us to know death.' On this cue Gerald enters; two pages have passed since he was last in the text, under the name of 'Cain'.

So 'everything hangs together', as Birkin had said; and the necessity that it should do so is behind Lawrence's emphasis on the novelty of his concept of form in fiction. Mere authenticity—the description of children, or the clothes at a fête—he could do as well as anybody; but in the matter of *hanging together* every book was a wholly new start. It is a view that Conrad, whom Lawrence never read well, would have shared; but the methods are different, and Lawrence's certainly implies a whole new approach to narrative. When the bodies are found it is Gerald's sister who has drowned the young doctor; the whole history of his family is used to strengthen the narrative myth of Gerald, and so are his fight with the mare, his use of the slave-girl Pussum, and finally, his self-destruction in the heart not of African darkness but of Alpine cold, the icy dissolution of the Northern races.

Another recurrence of great importance in the matching of doctrine and novel is the insistence on Birkin's sickness and on his occasional strident absurdity. Already when we encounter him at the Shortlands wedding party he is slightly ridiculous, gulping champagne and 'thinking about race or national death'. When he lectures Hermione in 'Class-Room' (III)—'We get it all in the head, really. You've got to lapse out before you can know what sensual reality is'—we are told that 'he sounded as if he were addressing a public meeting'. His attack on piano-owning colliers (V) is qualified by Gerald's patient smile; Gerald may be one of the damned, but he is allowed to register amusement when the saviour is silly. At Breadalby (VIII) the 'powerful, consuming, destructive mentality' which 'emanates' from Joshua (based on Russell) and Hermione (based on Lady Ottoline) also emanates from Birkin (based on Lawrence). Birkin feels he deserves Hermione's onslaught with the *lapis lazuli* paperweight, though her assault is quite firmly related to her corrupt voluptuousness.

Later, Ursula takes over the role of Birkin's critic; she cuts the metaphysic down to novelistic size. However near death she may herself feel, she instinctively rejects the apocalyptic excesses of Birkin. When he longs for a new world purged of humanity she is attracted by the notion but rejects it : 'she knew it could not appear so cleanly and conveniently. It had a long way to go yet, a long hideous way. Her subtle and demoniacal female soul knew it well' (XI). Humanity, says Birkin, 'rots in the chrysalis, it will never have wings'—the kind of diffuse doctrinal generalisation she can't stand, regarding it as venal immodesty, even as prostitution, since Birkin offered these essentially private meditations to all, indiscriminately : 'she hated the Salvator Mundi touch'.

'... what *do* you believe in?' she asked, mocking. 'Simply in the end of the world, and grass?'
He was beginning to feel a fool.
'I believe in the unseen hosts,' he said.
'And nothing else? You believe in nothing visible, except grass and birds? Your world is a poor show.'
'Perhaps it is,' he said ...

Birkin is like the canary which thinks night has come when somebody puts a cloth over its small cage.

The chapter called 'Moony' is famous as a doctrinal core, but it is worth looking at as an example of Lawrence's way of taming metaphysic by fiction. Ursula, finding the world 'lapsing into a grey wish-wash of nothingness', thinks well of cows, on the Whitmanesque grounds that 'they do not sweat and whine about their condition' (a famous passage in 'Song of Myself' which is followed by another about the stallion, which Lawrence must have still had in his head when he wrote *St Mawr*). In this mood of 'contemptuous ridicule' for humanity, she comes upon Birkin throwing dead flowers and stones into a pool, and muttering 'Cybele

—curse her! The accursed *Syria Dea*!' Not surprisingly she finds this ridiculous. But Lawrence is giving Birkin, in this silly situation, many essential things to say. Characteristically, therefore, he makes Birkin absurd at the outset, brings in his doctrinal critic, and then tackles the enormous task of leaping from absurdity to power. At once he writes the superb passage about the reflected moon, 'a white body of fire writhing and striving' as the stones shatter the surface of the water. Doctrine loses itself in pagan symbolism—the presence of the castrating moon-goddess may be shaken but not finally dispersed—and that, in turn, is lost in the virtuosity of the description of the interflow of light and dark on the water. Birkin and Ursula talk, combatively, differing about love; she wants surrender to it, he the equilibrium of separateness. Next day Birkin remembers Halliday's African statue, beetle-like, emblem of the sensual, of disintegration and dissolution: 'the principle of knowledge in dissolution and corruption'. The white races must undergo their version of the same process: 'ice-destructive knowledge, snow-abstract annihilation'. He thinks of Gerald, 'omen of the universal dissolution into whiteness and snow'.

This very complex passage is, of course, 'metaphysical', but it also depends upon the recurrence of the statue, and the anticipation of the last scenes of the book. It is so constructed that many of its expressions are untranslatable directly into narrative or, doctrine; what are the 'dreadful mysteries, far beyond the phallic cult', and what, in addition to our too mental, too abstract civilisation, is meant by the passage on racial death by frost? The whole thing has a deliberate afflatus, an incantatory haziness, as of apocalyptic preaching. Yet it is equally characteristic that Birkin switches his thought to a soul-equilibrium marriage with Ursula as an alternative to dissolution, and that he hurries over to her house to ask her to marry him. He is rejected; but Ursula, having fallen into a Gudrun-like contemptuous abstraction, swings round to the Birkin-view that human beings, 'painting the universe with their own image', are a blot on the true non-human universe. Yet she still wants of him complete surrender, abandon; while he seeks 'mutual union in separateness'. She is still bound by the false fleshly notions of the old Law, still unprepared for the new union of Law and Love. Birkin himself goes straight into 'Gladiatorial', his wrestling with Gerald, Gerald frictional, Birkin abstract, a strife for oneness between two men as different as man and woman, an exploration of intermediate sex and love which turns his thoughts back to Ursula : 'Gerald was becoming dim again, lapsing out of him.'

These chapters are full of metaphysic, but they transcend it; the risks they take are of implausible absurdity, and the power that enables Lawrence to take them successfully is the power not of a prophet but of a novelist, even in the matter of characterisation. For Ursula swings towards Gudrun, and Birkin to Gerald; then both achieve a certain release, and move together again. From what we know of them all we can, if we wish, interpret this allegorically, and up to a point the text encourages this. But not to the extent that we forget what Lawrence said in his letter to Garnett, and all the other things he says concerning the ways in which novels ought to shape themselves and their meanings. The metaphysic does not subdue, nor is it unchanged.

With Gudrun and Gerald, who do not directly voice or contest the metaphysic but are important in illustrating it, there are many instances of ambivalence. Gudrun is frictional, sensational, corrupted and corrupting; how well, with her high clanging metallic voice, her art, her interest in the marshy waterplants, her thrilled response to Gerald's imposing of his will on the mare, she complies with the theme of the river of dissolution. Yet she is also a charming girl, capable of intense sympathy with her sister, fond and even generous; it is she who saves the letter full of Birkinian metaphysic when Halliday and his friends are jeering at it in the Pompadour. As to Gerald, no occasion is lost of stressing his thematic significance : he is first described as having 'something northern about him'—'In his clear northern flesh and his fair hair was a glisten like sunshine refracted through crystals of ice' (I)—and we are continually reminded of this 'northern kind of beauty, like light refracted from snow' (XX). He first comes to Gudrun for love with churchyard clay on him, and the smell of dead flowers. Having imposed his will on the colliers as ruthlessly as on his mare, he stands with Gudrun under the railway arch where these corrupted victims of the mechanical dissolution make love to their girls. Gudrun has always been sexually excited by colliers. At their lovemaking 'she, subject, received him as a vessel filled with his bitter potion of death ... The terrible frictional violence of death filled her, and she received it in an ecstasy of subjection, in throes of acute, violent sensation' (XXIV). And he accepts her as Magna Mater, giver and renewer of his life.

Yet to find the house he had to ask the way of a stupid collier; and after this evil lovemaking he had, like any trivially illicit lover, to tiptoe downstairs at five in the morning, carrying his boots. Here, as in so many other of the pages concerning Gerald, we find, at the level of narrative, that union of the apocalyptic and the colloquial to which Kinkead-Weekes refers. Much of the same kind of thing may be said of the artist Loerke. He was in the early drafts, necessary to the racial aspect of Lawrence's apocalypse : a Jew, farther gone in corruption than the rest of us, a Chamberlain Jew, corruptly female, pederastic, devotee of the flow of dissolution. His views on art, hotly contested by Ursula, are powerfully opposed to life : decadent symbolism, the flesh represented geometrically, a Wyndham-Lewis-like cult of death. He is, as Birkin and Gerald agree, a rat, a beetle, all corrupt ego. At the last moment, Lawrence incorporated into his account of Loerke the 'terrible and dreadful' painting called 'The Merry-Go-Round' by his friend the Jewish artist Mark Gertler. He admired it, called it 'obscene ... but then, since obscenity is the truth of our passion today, it is the only stuff of art'. And he conjectures that Gertler is 'absorbed in the violent and lurid processes of inner decomposition ... It would take a Jew to paint this picture ... You are of an older race than I, and in these ultimate processes you are beyond me ... it will be left to the Jews to utter the great and final death-cry of this epoch ... But I think I am sufficiently the same, to be able to understand' (*C.L.* 477–8). Later Lawrence assured Gertler that Loerke was not he (*C.L.* 490); but there can be no doubt that he saw the picture in terms of his racial theory, and so associated it with Loerke. What is interesting is that in the book he arranges a conflict between this art of dissolution, and the art which is 'only the truth about the real world' (XXIX). Ursula tells Loerke that he is 'too far gone' to see that the second is the right one. The phrase is significant.

Gudrun is attracted to Loerke as to all manifestations of dissolution; he is illusionless, a 'mud-child. He seemed to be the very stuff of the underworld of life. There was no going beyond him.' He is in this sense reminiscent of the colliers who lust after Gudrun in her coloured stockings, and she feels excited by him. Yet this 'rat', this 'gnawing little negation', with his 'insect-like repulsiveness', is somehow made a man, and is the survivor in the clash with Gerald at the end. The scheme of the book called for a corrupt Jewish artist; the book makes that a wholly inadequate and 'metaphysical' description of the result. Loerke is important as an agent of the plot; satisfying Gudrun's lust for dissolution, he motivates her rejection of Gerald; he sends Gerald off into his own realm of death and icy corruption. He is important to the 'metaphysic'. But neither exigency can prevent his acquiring those qualities which belong to an art that has to do 'with the real world'.

Trust the tale, says Lawrence, and to make it trustworthy he gives us a Loerke whose connection with the 'metaphysic' is usually ignored; some critics even find him an admirable character. It is the same throughout. We could make a table of Birkin's beliefs and relate them very closely to Lawrence's views on the impending end, on race, on the complementary flows of creation and dissolution, on true marital relations as 'beyond love'—'star-equilibrium' (Carpenterian notion) with tension but no friction, spirit but no sensation. But the book does not exist to endorse these views; they are there in full strength, attended by the private system of images—rats, marsh, beetles and so on—but the text is neither messianic nor mechanical nor even conclusive.

What saves it from being any of those things is its honest insistence on its power to encompass absurdity, contradiction, tension. Its courage is remarkable. One scene after another—Birkin with the statuette in Halliday's flat, 'Gladiatorial'—tempts the absurd, but is forced through into meaning. Lawrence leaps precipitously from one emblematic scene to the next, chooses an image for his text and overwhelms it with a novelist's, not a preacher's passion. Consider 'Rabbit'. There is a clearly defined social situation : Gudrun is to be a teacher, her social situation is delicate; Winifred knows it. The French governess is envious or insolent. It might be a scene from a very conventional novel. But the rabbit Bismarck changes all that. There is a joke about cooking him, but he is a mystery, *ein Wunder*. Gudrun looks like a macaw, the governess is 'a little French beetle'. Bismarck is simply there to be drawn by the child. Then he exhibits his demoniacal power, a savagery that lacerates but satisfies Gerald and Gudrun. To make it work Lawrence had to use extreme imaginative force. Gerald brings 'his free hand down like a hawk on the neck of the rabbit'. Gudrun's seagull cry of excitement, the 'obscene recognition' that passes between her and Gerald, his obscene solicitude for her scratch, the reaction of the child, and the superb bit of dialogue which ends the chapter, are all the rewards of an artistic, not a prophetic risk.

Many such linked parables make the book—'The Chair', for instance. Occasionally we may find that matters have grown too simple (the representation, in 'Pompadour', of the old Café Royal as a 'small slow central whirlpool of disintegration and dissolution' is an instance of mental bombast, 'thoughts and images too great for the subject') but for the most part the writing is equal to the extraordinary demands made upon it. The chapter called 'Excurse' illustrates most of the risks and achievements. Here is the climactic struggle—starting in a newfangled car at the side of the road. Ursula accuses Birkin of deathly obscenity, of loving in Hermione both the sham spirituality and the foul sex-act: 'You are so *perverse*, so death-eating,' she says. They are interrupted by a passing bicyclist; and Birkin admits to himself his own degradation. She throws the jewels he has just given her—emblems of a warm creation —into the mud, and goes off, only to come back with a flower. That bicyclist is very typical of Lawrence. But the hardest part is to come: the love-scene in the Saracen's Head, her fingers tracing the life-flow in his thighs. At last she is a daughter of man with one of the Sons of God. From somewhere 'deeper than the phallic source' she gets the necessary knowledge of what lies beyond love and passion. They eat a large meal, plan the future, drive off (Birkin 'like an Egyptian Pharaoh, driving the car ... He knew what it was to have the strange and magical current of force in his back and loins, and down his legs, force so perfect that it stayed him immobile, and left his face subtly, mindlessly smiling'). Then they make love in a dark forest, giving each other 'the immemorial magnificence of mystic, palpable, real otherness'. However, they remember to send Ursula's father a telegram, to say she will not be home that night, and make a respectable excuse.

It is in such passages that Lawrence dares the reader to take the profound for the ridiculous; the bicyclist, the meal, the telegram, are all there to remind one that this is life, not a scribble to be resolved by reference to some doctrine, not a fantasy either. It is quite understandable that the intense insistence on Birkin's buttocks (a blend of sexual reverie and doctrine) strikes some as very ridiculous, and even sympathetic readers may feel some strain. But this is how he does it, and given that it was something so unprecedented, so strange, there was evidently no other way. Metaphysically Lawrence is saying (what he was soon to express in another doctrinal work) that the source of resistance to the evil male surrender to the solar plexus, the lapse into the hated mother, was in the lumbar ganglia; separateness once established and venerated, the 'immemorial magnificence' of that love-act was possible. It is not like the intentions of most novelists, and the method is therefore totally idiosyncratic.

The same is true of 'Continental', with its faintly comic presentation of a trip abroad as a great leap in the dark; it has to put the four principal characters into new relationships of great significance and complexity, and take many chances in the process. Yet this, and the concluding chapter, may be thought to represent Lawrence's power of complex narrative at its highest.

Of the acts of buggery in which all four characters appear to engage, two with benefit, two destructively, dissolutely—I shall say more in the pages on *Lady Chatterley's Lover*. Certainly they have something to do with the metaphysic : certainly in this version of Lawrence's apocalypse, it is necessary for those on the side of life to comply with dissolution in such a way that it is hard to distinguish them from the party of death. What is more important is the boldness with which Lawrence registers the schism between Gerald and Gudrun, the departure of Birkin and Ursula, and the encounter with the body of Gerald; that stiff body, its icy hair now literally frozen, glittering with frost. Birkin's 'He should have loved me,' and the final dialogue—the lovers parted again on the issue of the two kinds of love, the novel ending with its own equilibrium once more and finally disturbed—these belong to what Lawrence meant by the art of the novel. 'Philosophy, religion, science, they are all of them nailing things down, to get a stable equilibrium ... But the novel, no ... If you try to nail anything down, in the novel, either it kills the novel, or the novel gets up and walks away with the nail. Morality in the novel is the trembling instability of the balance. When the novelist puts his thumb in the scale, to pull down the balance to his own predilection, that is immorality ... And of all the art forms, the novel most of all demands the trembling and oscillating of the balance' (*P.I.* 528–9).

Women in Love has this instability. In life Lawrence was, it might seem, dangerously unstable at the time of its writing; but the book is unstable in exactly the sense he exigently demands of novels that are true, not false. The 'metaphysic' was important to him, and, as he believed, to everybody; he could not enact primary human relationships without putting it in. Yet to be effective it must not be programmatic; whatever got through to the reader would come not from the prescriptions of philosophy or religion, but from a sense of the beneficent instability of the text into which he wove it. The effort was so enormous that he was never to put it forth with quite the same energy again.

Chapter Two   1917–1921

[*Aaron's Rod, The Lost Girl*]

Lawrence's next novel in order of writing was *Aaron's Rod*, begun at the end of 1917, finished in September 1919, revised in 1920 and 1921, and published in the following year. Meanwhile he went on writing 'metaphysic': 'The Reality of Peace,' seven essays written in 1917, of which four survive; and 'The Education of the People' (late 1918). In 1919 he wrote *Psychoanalysis and the Unconscious* and, in the early summer of 1921, *Fantasia of the Unconscious*. Between these two books come the revised and completed pre-war novel now called *The Lost Girl*, and a new travel book *The Sea and Sardinia*.

The lack of impetus in *Aaron's Rod* has often been discussed; Lawrence put it aside several times, and in its present form it owes a good deal to the Italian journey he was at last able to make in late 1919. The first conception belonged to the war period, the black days of 1917 and 1918. Lawrence wanted to leave the country for Italy or for the U.S., which he hoped to find more apt for rebirth than Europe; though with *Sons and Lovers* in the 'scruple room' of the Boston Atheneum it is easy to imagine the fate of *Women in Love* had it appeared in those days. He was not allowed to leave 'the country of the damned', as he called England in a letter to Catharine Carswell: 'I curse England, I curse the English, man, woman and child, in their nationality let them be accursed and hated and never forgiven.'[1] The persecutions of the Cornish period fill the 'Nightmare' chapter of *Kangaroo*; Lawrence's hysteria, with its mixture of bullying and self-pity, reached a climax in September 1918, when, as the war neared its end, he underwent the compulsory medical examination described in *Kangaroo*.

The new novel did not, in these circumstances, fully engage his mind. He published *Look! We Have Come Through*, with its imagery of rebirth by sex from 'the sour black tomb'[2] and the poem *Manifesto*, celebrating the sexual achievement of 'having touched the edge of the beyond, and perished, yet not perished'. And the poet sought some further act 'on the root and quick of my darkness' whereby 'we shall be two and distinct, we shall have each our separate being ... Then we shall be free, freer than angels, ah, perfect.'[3] We have seen this desire reflected in *Women in Love*; and more will be heard of it. Indeed, at this very time, Lawrence in deep misery clung to the notion that the death-feelings he experienced were also the terrors preceding rebirth into a 'creative unknown' (*C.L.* 504)—that degradation was a necessary, though awful, preliminary. As usual, sexual experiment (including a strong friendship with a young Cornish farmer) was attended by much historical and prophetic speculation: the metaphysic went on developing, and Lawrence even wrote, on a surprising commission from Oxford University Press, a school history book, *Movements in European History*, which, in its peroration, advised the children that the future of Europe depended on their acceptance of 'a great chosen figure ... supreme over the will of the people'.[4] More striking still, he thought it proper to tell the children about the work of the Abbot Joachim of Fiora, whose *Everlasting Gospel*—published posthumously in 1254—divided history into three epochs—Father, Son and Holy Ghost—and spoke of the imminence of the Third Age.[5]

AARON'S ROD

The principle of Leadership, on which he had been meditating for some time, gets its first fictive expression in *Aaron's Rod*. For the framework of that fiction Lawrence depended rather shamelessly on the things that were happening, and the people he met, during its composition, on his Italian journey—Norman Douglas complains especially of the way the book (XII) rewards the hospitality of 'Sir William Franks' (*N*. II. 12). He grabbed at experience, incorporated it. The mountain scenery of Picinisco provided *The Lost Girl* with a climax totally unforeseeable when he began it. But there is nothing casual or fortuitous about the development of the metaphysic expressed, and occasionally criticised, in *Aaron's Rod*; its chief value is that it gives, with only a measure of ambiguity and reticence, an intelligible representation of Lawrence the prophet in the years between 1917 and 1921.

The book is rooted in the war, but contemplates a postwar Europe cheapened and debilitated—still at the end of an epoch rather than a beginning. Everything is tainted, from sexual relations down to food and drink. If the servants are dead so are their masters. The bohemian intelligentsia Aaron meets in London play with the idea of bloody revolution, or believe, in a trivial way, that Love can make them well again. The world is like a shell-shocked soldier, unhurt but wounded somewhere 'deeper than the brain' (*A.R.* X).

The story concerns Aaron Sisson, a miner who walks out on his wife and children one Christmas Eve and becomes a flautist in the Covent Garden orchestra; and Rawdon Lilly, a born leader, a separate man who serves without humility, and dominates without arrogance. Lilly, like Birkin, is often made to seem ridiculous; even the narrator calls him 'poor Lilly' (X) when he too vehemently declares that the war was simply an obscene mass-nightmare which never happened. One character, scorned beyond endurance by Lilly in what his wife calls his 'little Jesus' mood, strikes him; the opinions that had aroused Lilly's derision were that a man may seek salvation in the love and sympathy of a woman. Yet Lilly has power, and the text establishes it. 'Freak and outsider as he was,' Aaron reflects at the end, 'Lilly *knew*.

He knew, and his soul was against the whole world' (XXI). Nursing the sick Aaron, rubbing oil into his body, Lilly is represented as living in terms of an authentic style or code inaccessible to the masses, and this gives validity of a kind to his most fantastic or outrageously expressed opinions. Hence the situation at the end : Aaron is quite capable of contesting opinion, but he also recognises charisma; and the novel characteristically ends with him contemplating Lilly's face, 'like a Byzantine eikon', and considering not his love for the other man but his 'need to submit'.

Aaron himself is perhaps another aspect of Lawrence. He leaves his wife 'because I'm damned if I want to go on being a lover, to her or anybody' (VII); he is less opinionated than Lilly, but equally certain that the need for male separateness is not consistent with the love of woman. His flute enables him to survive alone, and is commended as a flexible, unmechanical, monodic instrument, as well as the emblem of male creativity. Lilly fights it out with his wife, Aaron simply and admirably departs. His wife had supposed herself 'as woman, and particularly as mother ... the first great source of life and being, and also of culture. The man was but the instrument and finisher ... It is the substantial and professed belief of the whole white world' (XIII). At this point the book, using Aaron's marriage as a text, begins to preach at us : the men of the white world accept these claims, 'conspire to agree that all that is productive, all that is fine and sensitive and noble, is woman. And however much they may react against the belief, loathing their women, running to prostitutes, or beer or *anything*, out of reaction against this great and ignominious dogma of the sacred priority of women, still they do but profane the god they worship. Profaning woman, they still inversely worship her'. Aaron, however, has a spirit which will not worship a woman. So he breaks into clean upright separateness, understanding that a man must not be given to a woman; when there is 'love consummation it must resemble Whitman's "Dalliance of Eagles", each bird borne on its own wings at the moment of ecstasy'. But given the age, the end of the long-drawn-out Christian epoch, Aaron is better without a woman.

These notions, expressed with virtually complete indifference to the form of the novel, are supported in various ways—by the complaint of the Marchese that his wife always retains the initiative in lovemaking (Aaron manages her better)—and, of course, in the explosions and disquisitions of Lilly. His friend Jim wants to recover from the war by indulgence in food and love, a sacrifice to the solarplexus. Lilly tells him to forget about love. 'Stiffen your backbone. It's your backbone that matters. You shouldn't want to abandon yourself' (VIII). It is after many such insults—'*You want to be loved*—a man of your years. It's disgusting'—that Jim attacks Lilly.

Lilly's disgust at the married state—'égoisme à deux! ... two in one—stuck together like jujube lozenges in little boxes' (XI)—is reflected in his struggles with his own wife; as a woman, confident of her superior role, she resists his natural authority over her. This resistance to authority has corrupted the world. The higher human types—Aztecs, Red Indians—disappear; the lower types—'Chinese, Japs and Orientals', flea-bitten Asiatics, Africans craven and cringing but bullies in the mass—these are the world now, when 'Man's spirit has gone out of' it (IX). Lilly's own salvation lies in strife—the fighting and passion that precede the condition of being together and apart in marriage. Strife will also be necessary in the world, men must fight, but not in the mass; they must assert their maleness and loneliness even in marriage. (Years later, according to Mabel Dodge Luhan, Lawrence advised her son on the eve of his marriage to be always alone, always separate, never to let his wife know his thoughts, to be gentle except when she opposed his will, when he was to beat her (*N*. II. 201).)

In the world at large socialism is merely a political manifestation of the epoch of Love; what is needed is 'a real committal of the life-issue of inferior beings to the responsibility of a superior being' (XX). Typically, Lilly responds to the objection of the man he's talking to by hedging, undercutting the megalomania; he has just stated his basic belief, which is in the inviolability and sacredness of the individual, when an anarchist bomb goes off and destroys Aaron's flute. Like the war, this bomb is love, 'only in recoil' (XXI). 'We've exhausted our love-urge, for the moment, And yet we try to force it to continue working. So we inevitably get anarchy and murder.' For Aaron the bombing of the flute is the end of an era, the sign that he must move into a newer and harsher one, an epoch of power in which there will be 'deep, unfathomable, free submission', especially by women. He replies with some scepticism to Lilly's final sermon; but the current of the plot is bearing him towards submission when the narrator's own scepticism ends the tale.

In the four years that had elapsed between the completion of *Women in Love* and that of *Aaron's Rod* we can see that the 'metaphysic', in so far as it shows through the novels, had hardened; its stridency is audible in the fiction, and it is being adapted more deliberately as a programme for action. Just as Ursula's rainbow was a false sign, so the apocalypse of *Women in Love* was a false apocalypse. The dissolution went on unchecked, its causes unchanged, and it showed no sign of giving way to some harsh renovatory process by the mere unaided action of apocalyptic history. The diagnosis of degeneration in the sexual relation could now achieve more forcible expression; male potency and separateness, the distrust of love because women and mothers control and own it, requiring male surrender, may be present in Birkin, but not in the same measure. And Loerke and Gerald are now practically the whole human race; mechanical, insect-like, it has survived the attempt to reduce it by extermination, and must simply be compelled into submission.

Given the tone of *Aaron's Rod*, it is not surprising that the writings on the 'metaphysic' which are contemporary with it are even harsher and more drastic in their recommendations. As early as 1915 he was telling Russell about the need for revolution, citing English sexual conduct as evidence (*C.L.* 317ff), but also urging the abolition of private property (*C.L.* 322), and contemplating action on behalf of the cause he and Russell, briefly, took up. But he told Russell he must drop his democracy. 'There must be an aristocracy of people who have wisdom, and there must be a Ruler' (*C.L.* 352). This belief grew if anything stronger while its concomitant—the need for the British to see that all hope lay in 'the adventure into the unexplored, the woman' (*C.L.* 319)—was much qualified. The doctrinal works of the *Aaron's Rod* period are very speculative, but do, in their way, attend to practical and political problems, for the most part providing extremely undemocratic, antilibertarian solutions.

THE REALITY OF PEACE; THE EDUCATION OF THE PEOPLE; FANTASIA; STUDIES IN CLASSIC AMERICAN LITERATURE

The Reality of Peace, however, begins by calling for abstinence from decision and the exercise of will; we must 'deliver our course to the current of the invisible' (*P.I.* 671). Thus we must pass through a crisis, into a new life, to which 'we must cede our will' (*P.I.* 674). We must undergo conversion, from death to life. This involves an acceptance of our darkness, of 'the flux of darkness and lively decomposition' (*P.I.* 676) in us, which we have formerly been ashamed of. The acceptance of corruption in the bowels, as a complementary stream to that of creation in the veins, is the condition of the new freedom; creation balances dissolution as spring balances autumn, and neither may be denied. Once we have accepted the serpent in the bowels we understand the interrelation of life and death, abolish shame, and pass beyond the duality of creation and dissolution into perfection, enter 'a new epoch of the mind' (*P.I.* 682). Failure to do so characterises human lives in periods of decadence. Death, then, must save us : 'Sweet, beautiful death, come to our help ... smash the glassy rind of humanity, as one would smash the brittle hide of the insulated bug. Smash humanity, and make an end of it. Let there emerge a few pure and single men ... Release me from the debased social body' (*P.I.* 693). The due expression of this transcendence is the man–woman relation, founded on love which draws them together and hate which keeps them separate : 'I am and I am not at once; suddenly I lapse out of the duality into a sheer beauty of fulfilment' (*P.I.* 694), like the earth peaceful in the grip of the attraction and repulsion of the sun.

Here the acceptance of corruption and death, hatred and violence, as a necessary condition of peace and fulfilment clearly stems from consideration of the sexual relationship (Lawrence's concern that its repulsions should include the excremental as a precondition of peace and stability I have already mentioned, and will again). The implication that few men can transcend, or even openly confess, this duality, is expressed in the shrill repetition of the earlier assault on human beetle-like corruption, the dismissal of humanity at large as irrelevant to creation or peace. But the people persist, and something must be done about them. They must be educated.

Birkin was an Inspector of Schools, though not, on the evidence, a very active one; Lawrence's next doctrinal work might have been written by him a few years later, had he in the meantime acquired, as Lawrence did, a brisk, repetitive, straight-from-the-shoulder journalistic manner; at its worst it sounds like Cassandra of the *Daily Mirror*. But behind it is a strong sense of the individual value of every person, and a passionate desire to separate the concept of the person from that of his job. His theory of education is designed to allow every child to develop its own uniqueness. Lawrence speaks as a 'board-school boy', and also as a board-school teacher, not as an Inspector, a university man, 'a refined soul down from Oxford'; he speaks as the socially inferior person who is nevertheless 'guardian of the high flame of human dignity' (*P.I.* 589). A small part of what he says, at the outset, would be endorsed without discomfort by educationists now. He deplores the attempt to make of the poor child a replica of the middle-class child, and the 'craven terror of poverty' that lies behind this (*P.I.* 591). Children who can't learn should not be taught. He suggests an examination at twelve, and 'streaming' thereafter, with the non-learners reduced to two hours a day of 'mental' education, plus three hours of physical and domestic training, until they are apprenticed at fourteen. The others will have more mental education, but they will not neglect physical and workshop training altogether. At sixteen there is another sorting process, allowing some to go to college, though still with an obligation to undergo physical and manual instruction. At twenty they go to graduate school, and at twenty-two issue forth as lawyers, doctors, priests, professors and so forth.

All education is paid for by the state, and all pupils take martial exercise, though without mechanical weapons. In this alone is education common to all; there is no concept of equality, except in that every person must be trained to fulfil himself according to his own nature. Teachers, 'the life-priests of the new era' (607), are employed not to do what God omitted to do, and make Jimmy Shepherd a Newton or a Shelley, but to foster 'spontaneous individuality in every man and woman' (606). The consequence will be a true caste system; degenerate democracy will be at an end without any revival of the soul-denying rigour of past hierarchical systems.

The legislation Lawrence requires is generous if not liberal in the ordinary sense; but as he develops his scheme the notion of the cultivation of uniqueness becomes more and more austere. For behind it is the notion, easily implanted in a man who has himself climbed educational ladders, that an inferior child will recognise its inferiority, and seek a master. Love, the odious source of democracy, has seduced us into theories of equality. The new era of the Holy Ghost will correct us. But how do people come to be as they are and as they must know themselves? The answer is that each man has a great solar plexus (sympathetic) which relates him to his mother, and a great lumbar ganglion (volitional), which, given its way, urges him towards individuality. The cardiac plexus is related to the solar, the thoracic to the lumbar. These are the centres of consciousness; mental operations are secondary. The solar plexus connects a man to his mother, via the navel; the lumbar ganglion urges him to stand free.

Lawrence's educational programme at this point becomes a simple requirement that the child be left alone. Mothers idealise and so exploit their connection with the solar plexus; they should be beaten for doing so. Mother love 'is a vice which threatens the ultimate sanity of our race' (622). It fosters affectations of various kinds, including idealism; damning self-conscious humanity, Lawrence wants 'spiritual, ideal self-conscious woman to be damned most of all' (631). So what is to be done, since we cannot all be suckled, as he says he would have preferred to be, by she-wolves? We must 'let go the upper consciousness' (633) and break the 'old yearning navel-string of love' (634) and be isolate and singular; we must 'set up the activity of the volitional centres' (639). This involves the care of the infant's backbone; it involves fierce behaviour, beatings on 'the centres of the primal will' (640): 'whipping, beating, yes these alone will thunder into the moribund centres and bring them to life' (641).

This is the teachers' job; they themselves should be 'of fine physical, motor intelligence, and mentally rather stupid' (644). They should cultivate in their pupils clear, exact movement, the sense of animal danger, emotional conflict. Thus they may learn to be alert, single, alone; they will also learn to be soldiers, 'hand-to-hand soldiers' (661). What kind of life can they have? Democracy will be discredited, so will the sacredness of the infant; most of all the prestige of women. Men and women, once the premental civilisation is founded, will be apart, meeting occasionally as on some suspension-bridge across a gulf. The man will tell the woman that he intends to get on with his business: 'Thinking, abstracting' (664). Women, who cannot do these things, will have to get on with their womanly activities, 'the immediate personal life'. The men scouting on ahead of their women, will form new relationships among themselves, cultivate 'greater abstractions, more inhuman activity' (665), forging a new kind of comradeship in 'these womanless regions of fight'. Marriage will be at the centre, friendship the leap ahead. And this is 'the last word in the education of the people'.

This latest development of the *Sons and Lovers* Preface is a strange and wild work; Lawrence wrote it, extraordinary as it may seem, with a view to publication in *The Times Educational Supplement*. It is not difficult to see how it grew from his earlier speculations, nor, for that matter, does he trouble to conceal its relation to his personal history: there had to be a theory which could explain his mother, Miriam and Frieda. What is surprising, though, is that the repeated injunction to leave the child alone applies mostly to women, and means simply that love should not be expressed. Teachers have no difficulty about love; and the 'spanking' of children, so oddly justified, is a subject which excites Lawrence a little more than the theory explains. It is a topic which crops up again and should not be ignored by explorers of Lawrence's psychology. It is also a reminder that extreme radicalism, however divorced from practicality, is often violent; and that totalitarian politics whether successful or not have rarely been pacifistic.

Perhaps it would be wrong to exaggerate the novelty of Lawrence's ideology. He is one of a great crowd of thinkers who have held to the notion that there is a consciousness other than the mental, and that modern civilisation has repressed it; this is one of the basic modern myths (a word which does not suggest that it is untrue any more than 'modern' means that it has not a long history). That the disastrous pressures of civilisation are accountable for the unsatisfactory nature of our sexual relations, or that civilisation is achieved only at the expense of distorting our sexuality, is a view associated with Freud and with Reich, who placed the blame firmly on 'the authoritarian family'. Lawrence's solution is of course almost the opposite of Reich's, which is orgastic and anti-patriarchal and anti-authoritarian; Lawrence had a deep distrust of female orgasm, wanted male domination in the family, and—at this stage—political dictatorship. These differences characteristically arise in the superstructure of such thinking. Whereas Freud, especially in the early *Project*, used for heuristic purposes fictions which were founded on science, and Reich developed a pseudo-science of orgone energy, Lawrence did his thinking in antiscientific, occult terms; the story of the sympathetic and volitional centres merges into that of the *chakras*; soon he will take a 'sudden lurch into cosmology, or cosmogony' (*Fantasia* 53). The machinery of his system grows more and more complex, generating new thoughts as well as explaining old ones. But it is the same basic insight that is elaborated, whatever the fictive form adopted.

In *Psychoanalysis and the Unconscious* (1921) and *Fantasia of the Unconscious* (1922) Lawrence explains his developing views, and distinguishes them from Freud's. In terms of the history of ideas, Lawrence operates a 'soft'

primitivism, Freud a 'hard' one; Lawrence wants an innocent unconscious, not a 'cellar in which the mind keeps its
own bastard spawn' (*Psy.* 9), as he says of Freud's; he argues
that the horrors of the Freudian unconscious are propa-
gated by mental intervention in sex. And he outlines again
the navel-centred psychology of the baby, 'negatively polar-
ized' (23) by 'the great ganglion of the spinal system', which
works for 'sundering, separation'. In sex it is of the utmost
cultural importance that these drives, 'the sympathetic and
separatist' (40) should remain in tension. The old dualism is
expanded, first into four 'centres', two above, two below
the waist, and then in the closing passage into 'seven planes'
(49). But although these extensions allow the argument to
be differently expressed (and correspond, in their different
way, to the enlargement of the Freudian scheme) the
thought remains much the same: the need for self-realisa-
tion, the need to break away from the ruinous tyranny of
'idealism'. It is the 'philosophy' of *Aaron's Rod*.

Fantasia continues the argument, but more speculatively.
Proceeding intuitively, but after readings in 'the Yoga and
Plato and St John the Evangel and the early Greek philoso-
phers like Herakleitos down to Frazer ... and even Freud
and Frobenius', Lawrence seeks to recapture a science older
than the dead mechanistic modern variety; universally
taught, it belonged to the Glacial Period when the seas were
dry, and 'men wandered back and forth from Atlantis to
the Polynesian Continent'. Lawrence was not, in his day or
ours, alone in supposing that lost myth and symbol were
ripe for rediscovery; that we have a racial memory of
images belonging to the science that ruled before the great
Flood that divided the continents. He will attempt 'to
smatter out the first terms of a forgotten knowledge' (54–6).

The emphasis is again on the individual's uniqueness,
identified with the Holy Ghost, reconciler of the mother
and father in him. The mother, via the solar plexus, en-
forces a sympathetic relation with the cosmos; the father,

via the lumbar ganglion, separateness. The rest, though varied in expression, is mostly familiar. The father will 'spank' because 'the vibration of the spanking acts directly upon the spinal nerve-system ... the spanker transfers his wrath to the great will-centres in the child, and these will-centres react intensely, are vivified and educated' (88). This, and the suppression of mental consciousness, are the new educational programme; the schools are now to be closed down altogether. Boys must be boys, girls girls. The second of these recommendations requires that women no longer 'act from an idea' (121); Eve did that, and so we lost Paradise and 'got our sex into our head'. Consequently, 'the whole man-and-woman game has become just a hell' and we have only two choices : to pass on, and leave room for another race; or to get rid of the disease, called 'mental consciousness' or 'self-conscious idealism' or 'love' (122). Education being the way in which this disease reaches the masses, it is important to deprive them of it; they will soon 'instinctively fall into line' with the new order. Girls domestic, boys martial, they will all obey the Leader. They will be denied all knowledge of sex until after puberty, except what they see for themselves; but, strong in exclusive maleness and femaleness (there is no intermediate sex (131) will avoid that mental disaster which makes women the rulers. Then sex will again be rebirth for the full man; his night-experience after the adventures of the day. Homosexuality and masturbation (always treated by Lawrence, as by Reich, with disgust) are consequences of our failure to maintain this polarity, our sell-out to 'love'. Other consequences are 'beastly benevolence, and foul good-will, and stinking charity, and poisonous ideals' (174) and war.

The cosmological fictions achieve fullest expression on Chapter XIII of the *Fantasia*; there is no point in summarising them, since their purpose is not to say what the world is like in fact, but to establish that the universe is organic, that the sun corresponds to the solar plexus and the moon, a

thing of 'almost malignant apartness ... frictional separation', to the lumbar ganglia (192). Dreams are also given
organic significance : dreams of crawling through narrow
passages relate to the movement of blood in the arteries. A
terrifying dream about horses has nothing to do with a
'father-complex'—the rearing horse is the image of the
sacral ganglion, the spontaneous self seeking liberation
from the 'automatic pseudo-soul' (199) which represses it.
So powerful is the need to respect day- and night-conscious-
ness (the one dominated by the eye, the other by the blood)
that we should never stay up late or rise late, keeping time
with the moon and sun, and allowing, in the darkness, the
polarised bloodstreams of man and woman to meet in 'pure
frictional crisis' (202). Thus, when his refreshed blood runs
back into its channels, the man is reborn after the labours
of the day. The true woman has a downward flow of consciousness to loins and belly—if you pervert it you get 'intelligent' women, mere female companions, or prostitutes,
not that polar opposite by contact with which a man re-
news himself in a sexual conflict beyond love. Woman's
business is at night; by day she is to sit 'half in fear' of the
man, submitting to a purpose which is 'beyond her'. The
book ends on these fairly familiar recommendations.

Lawrence jeers at, flouts his reader, telling him he can
please himself whether he believes all this; it is part of his
instinctive defence against ridicule. And there is no point, I
think, in denying that there is a deal of rubbish in the *Fantasia*. Dr. Leavis is surely exceeding reason and balance in
asserting that it 'has ... the poise of lucid and sober intelligence'[6] without explaining why, in this case, it smothers
its basic theme in angry nonsense which the author will not
even stand by. The value of the works is not in their recommendations about education or the subjection of woman, or
in their physiology or cosmology, but in their tormenting
insistence on every man's responsibility to his own uniqueness, on the possibility of his regeneration, on his finding his

own vital relation to the world. But 'art speech is the only speech', as Lawrence observed, and he spoke fully only when speaking it. His mind needed strenuous engagement with art, with a text, or at least with recollected experience, before it could achieve the complex expression it needed; we have already seen him engage his own and others' art in this way. That is why *The Sea and Sardinia*, written immediately before the *Fantasia* in 1921, is so much more satisfying than the purer flight of 'metaphysic'. It contains a good deal of doctrine of all sorts (propaganda for capital punishment and marital strife; contempt for the 'dark' races; lamentations for the extinct quality of maleness; admiration for the more savage of our contemporaries, who expect no gentleness, no love; rejoicings that 'the era of love and oneness is over' (91); yearnings for the final destruction of the evil power of women) but it also speaks of meat and vegetables and fruit, of people and places, with the responsive quickness, the sensitive colour and line which are what in the end convince us that the man is to be attended to.

One of the triumphs of the doctrine occurred, characteristically, when Lawrence brought a mind full of it, but still almost supernaturally quick in its response to life, here the life of a set of texts, to his critical work on American literature. During the war, mostly in Cornwall, he had been reading the American novelists and Whitman as a preparation for his hoped-for journey to the New World. Between August 1917 and February 1919 he wrote a dozen essays on these themes, eight of which were published in the *English Review*. He revised them drastically in Sicily (1920) and again in New Mexico in 1922–3, to produce the version published in 1923 as *Studies in Classic American Literature*. The earlier version was published in 1962 as *The Symbolic Meaning*.

This version, though much less known and relatively hard to obtain, is much the finer. In revision Lawrence understandably altered some of his views: he now knew America, and the substitution of reality for myth meant some tempering of his praise, some changes in his judgments, even the introduction of a contemptuous note. What is almost totally harmful in the recasting of the work is the new tone of jeering journalism, and a sort of hysteria which Mr Armin Arnold, who edited the earlier versions, attributes to the nervous tension of Lawrence's life in Taos. Certainly the ambiance of Mrs Luhan was almost the worst imaginable for a writer of Lawrence's kind, already prone to nervous frenzies. Whatever the cause of the change of tone, the first version best illustrates how metaphysic could assist Lawrence's intellectual operations.

To Lawrence the Americans are strangers, and their literature cannot be considered apart from their place, the land from which they see and feel the world. His subject is 'difference and otherness' (17). American writers have sought to conceal that otherness, but their 'art speech' gives them away: that is why we have to listen to that, to the tale and not to the teller. Already, by the late war years, Lawrence thought of art speech—imaginative fiction—as 'a language of pure symbols', the 'greatest universal language of mankind' (18–19). The critic's job is to listen to this language, not to its author. In so doing Lawrence proved himself a critic of exceptional power.

For him the visible America is only a monstrous development of the old Europe, a product of the overdeveloped will, a mechanical democracy; but there remains under that false America a true one, slowly emerging—an Indian not a paleface America, which will express the land as its beasts and flowers express it. While we wait for the birth of this America we can study the progress of its white counterpart, which is transmuting men into machines and ghosts. There is Franklin, insentient to the living universe, 'the gleaming Now' (40), slave of the will he cultivated, enemy of the mystery of the Self. There is Crèvecœur, rich in sensual understanding, capable of a 'primal dark veracity' (65), half in love with the Indian, with a tension between his idealism and his art that illustrates the dualism of Lawrence's great nerve-centres. Fenimore Cooper calls forth another lecture on the solar plexus and lumbar ganglia, an early allusion to St John's Revelation as an allegory of the conquest of the sensual centres by the dynamic consciousness, and another to the Eleusinian mysteries. Cooper hints at American re-birth, the communion of white and red, the new 'race-soul' (103). The essays on Cooper are an astonishing achieve-ment, a delicate, rapt symbolic interpretation of material few would have thought to promise much to an approach of this kind.

With Poe disintegration takes firm hold. He illustrates the process, which can in its way be beautiful, of dissolution. This is also part of the theme of the fine Hawthorne essay, so debilitated in the later version. It begins with the asser-tion that the primary or sensual mind progresses from myth to art, the reasoning mind from ancient cosmic theory to science; when these two are reconciled man can live in his fullness. Meanwhile the nearest approach to a union is in art. Hawthorne illustrates the gap; 'there is a discrepancy between his conscious understanding and his passional understanding' (138). In *The Scarlet Letter* his attempt to be rational fails, and the book gives us, in spite of him, 'the passional or primary account of the collapse of the human psyche in the white race' (139), distorted in the same way as alchemy and astrology are distorted remains of an old knowledge of the organic universe. Thus Haw-thorne's book, but not Hawthorne, recovers an ancient mode of sensual understanding, and Lawrence praises it un-reservedly. Hawthorne's ethical intrusions, he insists, are precisely what the critic must discount. Trust the tale.

Sometimes the metaphysic stifles the intuitions, as when, in writing of Dana, Lawrence approves the flogging of the sailor as good for the lumbar-sacral ganglia of the victim, even if he has a 'smarty back' (202), and good for the captain, too, as proof that he's master. But this rarely happens, even in the demonstration that *Moby Dick* symbolises the apocalyptic destruction of 'sacral-sexual consciousness' (235). Lawrence detests Melville's conscious symbolism; 'his mind lags far, far behind his physical comprehension' (237). But *Moby Dick*, as felt by Lawrence, still sounds like 'one of the strangest and most wonderful books in the world'.

Finally Whitman, 'the greatest of the Americans' (254) and indeed 'the greatest modern poet' (264). Lawrence had over the years absorbed a good deal of Whitman; but now he sees him as ushering in the last stage of the reduction of the sensual to the spiritual, a process begun by Christianity and now reaching its end. Like the other moderns—French, Russian, English—he had art in the head. He conquers 'the lower centres' (257). He is the climax of the dying epoch of Love; he it is that captures the whale, 'the pure sensual body of man' (259–60). Whitman was wrong in making women purely functional—muscles and wombs—but right in stressing the importance of man acting womanless : 'the polarity is between man and man. Whitman alone of all moderns has known this positively' (261). The relationship between males is beyond marriage though it must coexist with marriage. The new epoch Whitman heralds will be one of the love of comrades. By the time Lawrence wrote his final version of the essay he had changed his mind about comrades, and jeered at Whitman for believing in them, and in the future : 'This awful Whitman. This post-mortem poet.' Yet, for all his mistakes, his identification with Love, Whitman remains 'the first white aboriginal' (173) of America, the bearer of the necessary heroic message.

There are tiresome and even silly things in this book; but in its penetration of the texts, its concern for the spirit of place, it is a justification of the metaphysical fictions by which Lawrence did much of his thinking. The literary criticism is made part of the pattern of all his other interests. The later version of the book retains some of the good things from the earlier, and makes some points more precisely; but in shedding much of the metaphysic it acquires a chill sneering tone, and is often hideously written. The loss is great; though some romantic notions are excised—for example the confidence that white men could be turned into Indians was qualified by Lawrence's experiences in New Mexico—there is a baser kind of knowingness which is no gain. Basically the scheme is the same, and the Joachite Holy Ghost still presides:

> *The Father had his day, and fell.*
> *The Son has had his day, and fell.*
> *It is the day of the Holy Ghost.* (109)

Lawrence had learnt his own system. In some ways he makes it more flatly explicit: 'the Pequod was the ship of the white American soul. She sank ...' (160). And Whitman, constantly heckled, remains 'a very great poet, of the end of life' (170). *Studies in Classic American Literature* was still a powerful enough book to change the ways in which a nation reads its classics. So much for the utility of the 'metaphysic'.

The American studies are the culminating work of this second period; it remains to say a brief word about the rest of the fiction that falls within it. This consists mainly of the stories collected in *England, My England* (1923), the three long stories published in *The Ladybird* (1923) and the novel, *The Lost Girl*. The earliest of the long stories is *The Fox*, a work remarkable for the success with which Lawrence uses the fox-symbolism in a situation which is full of 'metaphysical' possibilities realised only in that symbolism, and in the surrender of the tale to a sort of mute expressiveness; there is no discursive doctrine, nothing intrusive. *The Lady-bird* contemplates aristocracy and war ('the years when the old spirit died for ever in England'); Count Dionys is full of

Lawrentian prayers against an insufferably mechanised humanity ('Beat, hammer of God, beat them down') and a worshipper of the necessary destruction, the aristocratic Lawrentian anarchist. But dangerous as the situation sounds, art-speech prevails, even when the topic of conversation is the Principle of Decomposition; for the ladybird symbol controls it. *The Captain's Doll* is justly given extended treatment by Dr Leavis;[7] it is one of the strangest and most ambiguous of the stories, but as a tale it is too much for its author.

THE LOST GIRL

The Lost Girl, begun in 1913, opens in a manner inescapably reminiscent of Arnold Bennett, a reaction to *Anna of the Five Towns* (1912). It starts with an account of a draper's shop in a small Midland town. Originally called *The Insurrection of Miss Houghton*, it scrupulously chronicles the revolt, within culturally permissible limits, of a girl born in that milieu. It is, in part, a demonstration of the ease with which Lawrence used the skills he knew he must renounce. Breaking away from the stifling menage of a foolish father, Alvina becomes a midwife; she is dragged back, but eventually escapes. The text has a certain matey discursiveness: 'Our mothers pined because our fathers drank and were rakes. Our wives pine because we are virtuous but inadequate. Who is this sphinx, this woman? Where is the Oedipus that will solve her riddle of happiness and then strangle her?—only to marry his own mother!' (IV). This is straight from the *Sons and Lovers* foreword. Elsewhere, characters unexpectedly voice Lawrentian views on education. But the tale has both subtlety and drive, as when Alvina goes down a mine and encounters the humiliated body and dark blood-knowledge of the miner. Although her need for a new life is not immediately supplied, there is just enough indication of its possibility to keep her from sinking into the society of stereotypes about her. Her father opens a sort of cinema-music-hall, an absurdity which gives Alvina her chance, for she falls in with an 'Indian' troupe of travelling players. (Lawrence borrowed this idea, presumably, from *Hard Times*.) These bizarre second-rate artistes retain a contact with the instinctual life that the respectable have lost. Their probable rejection by the public in favour of films seems to him further proof of the destructiveness of that new mechanical medium, flickering, dreamlike, unsocial to the point of being nothing but a means of driving people into their own mean fantasies, into masturbation; an entertainment suitable only to workers spiritually destroyed by machines.

Alvina, pianist at the show, falls in with an Italian member of the troupe. Cicio is superficially a rather low Neapolitan *ragazzo*, but underneath there is a Lawrentian male, black-eyed, dominant, blood-conscious. Alvina joins the troupe and after many adventures marries Cicio; they go off to their Italian mountain solitude, where she is left when Cicio goes to war.

This last part of the book owes much to Lawrence's elopement, and has some of that travelogue quality which Lawrence also allowed into *Aaron's Rod* and some later novels. But there is a rightness in the design; the total rejection of an England to which, in Bennett's *The Old Wives' Tale*, Sophie eventually has to return, the sense of a latent life going on behind its smoky deadness. If the narrative sometimes verges on silliness (as in Cicio's serenading Alvina as she attends a woman in labour) it also renders very subtly the expense of spirit in Alvina's father, his odd sprightliness reduced by the universal necessity of mechanical selling, and in the shabbiness of the troupe. The mountains at the end are firm, imaginatively placed, and truly resolve the story.

It was possible for Katharine Mansfield, who loved and hated Lawrence, to detest *The Lost Girl* for its triviality and falsity—she cites the scene in which Alvina makes love with Cicio and goes back singing to the washing-up, as well as that of the woman in labour (*N*. II. 52). And it is true that there is a lack of tension in the book, a less passionate involvement with the tale. Its beginning is pre-*Rainbow*, its end belongs to another period of transition; the war interrupted it, and so changed the author that he would not, presumably, have chosen to begin where it began. The metaphysic leaves enough marks on *The Lost Girl* to make it easily identifiable as Lawrence's work, though it is by no means as assertive as in *Aaron's Rod*. This is not wholly a bad thing, but it does indicate that the text did not deeply engage him; and the book also lacks the marks of the struggle which make both *Women in Love* and the American essays, in their different ways, such distinctive indications of his genius.

Chapter Three 1922–1925

[*Kangaroo, The Boy in The Bush, The Plumed Serpent, St Mawr*]

KANGAROO

Early in 1922, the Lawrences went east, stopping briefly in Ceylon on the way to Australia. Between April and August, when they left for New Mexico, they lived rootlessly in a country Lawrence found interesting, though in the end lacking the possibility of a new life. In June and July he wrote *Kangaroo*, adding a final chapter on arrival in New Mexico. Hastily written and often very flat, *Kangaroo* is nobody's choice for Lawrence's masterpiece, but it has a special interest. Lacking that process of creative revision by which Lawrence complicated his texts and himself, it offers a surprisingly naked self-portrait, a record of fact and un-censored fantasy not elsewhere to be found. His Australian admirer Katherine Susannah Pritchard protested against its acceptance as 'an authentic picture of Australia'; Lawrence, by his own admission, knew very little about it, 'felt blind to it', as Somers says in the book, and was especially ignorant about its democratic politics (*N*. II. 154–5). Later Australian criticism somewhat qualifies this judgment: the politics in the novel, though fantasticated and inadequate, are not altogether remote from those of contemporary Australia. There was a conflict between a sociaist move-ment and a para-fascist 'digger' movement, and Lawrence related it, 'weirdly', as he said himself, to his current specu-lations about authority in the home and in the state.[1] He called the book a 'thought-adventure' (XIV). The story gropes forward, interrupted by sermons of which 'the re-cord was taken down for this gramophone of a novel'.

Lawrence was not the kind of person who likes Australia; for all his indignant rejection of them he soon felt nostalgia for England and 'lovely Europe', and he had what can only be called a middle-class contempt for the 'colonial'. Thus it is not surprising to discover that in spite of his powerful reaction to the primeval strangeness of the landscape and fauna—beautifully registered in the book—he at once hated the democratic manners, the vulgar friendliness of the people, so that as it seemed to him a worn-out second-hand civilisation had been dumped ridiculously down on the unimaginably old squat inhuman forms of the continent. Thus there was no new life, only a life 'one step farther gone into dissolution' than that of the parent country. Not surprisingly, the people and politics of whom he professed to be writing did not engage him at any deep level; he wrote on and on without cease, even when uncertain of what to do next, included a whole chapter of earlier autobiography, and even wrote one chapter called 'Bits' (XIV), of which several pages are simply copied out of the Sydney *Bulletin*. 'Chapter follows chapter', he observes at the opening of XV, 'and nothing doing.' Apart from the descriptions, the main interest of the book is as a record of the opinions and fantasies of Lawrence at the moment of writing.

Hence it would be unreasonable to dismiss as merely intrusive the famous chapter called 'The Nightmare' (XII). Recounting the experiences of the war years—including the expulsion from Cornwall and the climactic medical examination—it serves to explain his Australian mood. He grew more and more fond of Christ's words *noli me tangere*—do not touch me—(especially because they were addressed to a woman), and the experience of having doctors handle his private parts and peer up his anus was the most intolerable of his life. 'Never would he be touched again. And because they had handled his private parts, and looked into them, their eyes should burst and their hands should wither and their hearts should rot' (XII). Brought up in working-class society with its promiscuous social contacts and neglect of privacy, he still had an instinct for that kind of life, or a refined version of it; but some forms of contact were too intimate, and he rejected them as he rejected his mother. He admired 'the gulf' between the native servants and the whites' in India (II); he made Somers shrink from his friend Caldecott when he hugged him; and as much as the 'vacancy' of Australian freedom he hated Australia's messy equality and proletarian manners. 'They are ten times more foreign to me ... than Italian scoundrels, or even Indians ... And yet their manner of life, their ordinary way of living is almost exactly what I was used to as a boy' (VII).

'The Nightmare' had changed him, confirmed him in a loathing for 'the filthy-mouthed *canaille*', a touchy, isolate pride, that made him a bad visitor to Australia. Somers-Lawrence looks a gentleman, 'sensitive all over' (IV), a natural aristocrat, especially compared with Australians. This is the explanation of the intolerable rages, meannesses, sillinesses, for which Harriet (Frieda) and, it must be said, the narrative, continually chide and deride him. The book is basically about the muddle his passion for separateness gets him into. On principles already established he ought to be seeking a creative male world beyond marriage; but he cannot join other men, his direction is 'Back to the central self, the isolate, absolute self' (XIV), remote not only from the soulless masses, but from all men, even those who attract him. He thinks of isolation as the only good—'a man alone with his own soul : and the dark God beyond him'; but it seems clear that implication in 'the horrible human affair' cannot be avoided by one who seeks the new age; action, cooperation, leadership are required. And the fantasy of Lawrence, the leader of men, on which *Aaron's Rod* came to its uncertain close, is critically explored in *Kangaroo*.

First he must dominate his wife; and *Kangaroo* records the ensuing marital conflict. Somers cannot have an easy permissive Australian love-marriage; he wants monogamy and mastery. 'You can't have two masters in one ship,' he says; Harriet 'was to submit to the mystic man and male in him' (IX). He quite understands why Harriet contemptuously refuses to do so; he is not yet worthy, has not yet opened 'the doors of his soul and let in a dark Lord and Master for himself' (IX). He knows he is still cursed with mother-love, whether his real mother's in dreams, or Harriet's.

In this condition he cannot act, cannot yield to the male temptations of political action. He certainly cannot identify his own apocalypse or utopia with that of socialism, and hesitates to identify his authoritarianism with that of the Digger movement, led by Kangaroo. This is the oddest and perhaps the most profound issue in the book. Kangaroo is a strange *doppelgänger* for Lawrence—a viserotonic Jew, very loving, who is finally shot and dies in the stink of dissolution. Why did Lawrence do this? He approved of the militarist racism of the movement (though significantly a crucial conversation about this is made absurd because both speakers have to shout against the noise of the sea). He believed in submission to a leader; but he makes the leader an emotional Jew, who offers him a mystic male union. Somers declines: 'Not blood-brotherhood. None of that' (VI). Birkin's desire he no longer feels, at any rate for this man. Yet he likes him, even for his Jewishness 'the very best that is in the Jewish blood: a faculty for pure disinterestedness, and warm, physical warm love' (VI). And he accepts the Kangaroo position that men need a father rather than a suffering saviour, though an obsession with Law (as represented by Woman) is, on another view, exactly what is wrong with the Jews. He will even accept Kangaroo as a kind of god, and contemplate a union between them: kangaroo and tiger rather than lion and unicorn, the fat and the thin, the outgoing and the isolate, solar plexus and sacral ganglia divided between two persons. But although Kangaroo is a son of man, he loves not woman but Man; Harriet turns against him, and Somers rejects him, refusing to risk love of any kind. Kangaroo can't see that the advent of a new epoch is a move on from Love, that first there is darkness ('it is time for the Son of Man to depart and leave us dark, in front of the unspoken God' (VII)). So Somers rejects Kangaroo's love, can even watch him die without admitting that he loves him. Taking the lumbar stance, he won't give in to the solar plexus. Harriet thinks all this is hot air; Kangaroo thinks it is murder. Politically, Somers predicts that the conflict of Diggers and socialists will now ruin the love-ideal, and produce chaos. But this is what he wanted. If the Leader, ruling by 'vertebrate telepathy' a society held together by his charisma— by vibrations emanating from him as they did from Napoleon, and as they do in animal societies—if the Leader fails, as Lawrence partly knew he would—there must, before the unimaginable new age of preconscious isolate unanimity, be a chaos, a bloodbath. At moments he quite looked forward to it.

Somers left Australia, that 'vast continent … devoid of speech' (XVIII) so horrible in its machine civilisation, because it emphasised his impotence. It was as hateful as the old Europe, still existing 'under the withered, repulsive weight of the Hand of the Lord, that old Jew' (XVIII). Only the bush was satisfyingly manless, unfriendly, beautiful. Somers-Lawrence must depart, to continue the search for some place where he could reconcile his apocalypticism with his scepticism.

THE BOY IN THE BUSH

Kangaroo shows Lawrence, though passionate in other respects, as nearly as possible careless of what he was doing in his narrative; Chapter IX is perhaps the worst writing in the whole canon. Yet finally the book is well worth the attention of anybody trying to understand him. And so is the other, somewhat neglected, Australian novel, *The Boy in the Bush.* Lawrence rewrote an original novel by an Australian nurse, Mollie Skinner, an act of collaboration that may seem surprising, but is in its way characteristic; the business of rewriting was to Lawrence quite as creative as that of writing. He seems to have confined himself to alterations in the texture, and the smuggling in of his thoughts on male supremacy and Australian inferiority, except in the final chapters, which were entirely changed (*N.* II. 274ff.). Later it transpired that Lawrence originally made the hero die, but Frieda, thinking this another piece of male chauvinism, compelled him to alter it. ' "Let him become ordinary," I said. Always this superiority and death' (*N.* II. 355). Lawrence found in the Boy another congenial double, realising his own passional hopes in the virgin bush, commending blood-knowledge : 'Vision is no good ... words are no good ... we must communicate with the arrows of sightless, wordless knowledge, as Jack communicated with his horse, by a pressure of the thighs and knees' (XXVI). Jack is isolate, and will never give himself away except in momentary weakness to a woman (never a black woman). Bigamy is a possibility; but first he must become a Lord of Death, knowing the spiritual by the passional body, 'drunk with the sun and moon' (XII). Thence proceeds 'masterhood' (XXIII); the Lord of Death is the Lord of Life. So he solves the spiritual dilemma brought on by the fear of death he experiences early in the book. His children will be a new race, 'with a new creed of courage and sensual pride, and the black wonder of the halls of death ahead, and the call to be lords of death on earth' (XXV). They will be born of marriages that have nothing to do with 'this soft and hideous thing called love ... he would have love in his own way, haughtily, passionately, and darkly, with dark, arrowy desire, and a strange arrowily-submissive woman' (XIX). In the end he finds one, and departs on his 'ruddy, powerful horse' into the bush 'in which he had once been lost' (XXVI).

The Australian interlude was in its way productive. The theories and fantasies of *Aaron's Rod* were developing into a primitivist mythology of telepathic leadership which the experience of New Mexico and Mexico were to extend. Lawrence remained in New Mexico from September 1922 till September 1925, with interruptions for visits to Mexico and England. This time, spent largely under the aegis of Mabel Dodge Luhan at Taos, is a distressingly well-documented period of his life. The country suited Lawrence better than any he had found, but life in 'Mabeltown' was so ridiculous and petty that it was a continual exasperation to his pride, and his own conduct in turn did much to make the situation worse. Nevertheless these were productive years. *The Plumed Serpent* was written in 1923, and revised two years later; *The Woman Who Rode Away*, *The Princess* and *St Mawr* belong to 1924–5, and the sketches collected in *Morning in Mexico* to the same period. He also produced additions to the metaphysic, and some journalism. In the summer of 1925 he wrote some important essays on the novel. Earlier that year he suffered an almost fatal illness, and began a novel called *The Flying Fish*, of which a fragment survives (P. I. 78off.).

The metaphysical explorations are best represented by 'Him with the tail in his Mouth' (P. II. 427ff.) which, in the jeering tabloid prose Lawrence had developed for such work—witness the definitive version of *Studies in Classic American Literature*—speaks again of that fourth dimension in which all things have their plural, separate and immortal being, and of the Holy Ghost as the patron of this timelessness, presiding over this total harmony, reconciling the polarity of man and woman. What must be given up to achieve this peace—the Reign of Love in favour of the Reign of Power, decadent notions of the equality of men and races in favour of natural and voluntary subordination—is the theme of the pieces he added to *The Crown* in order to make up the book called *The Death of the Por-*

cupine (1926). *Mornings in Mexico* (1927) is more interesting. Lawrence found in the Indians that true primitive pantheism which insists that the mind is 'merely a servant, to keep a man pure and true to the mystery' ('Indians and Entertainment') and celebrated this sanity in 'Dance of the Sprouting Corn' and 'Hopi Snake Dance', two of his most spectacular primitivist setpieces. Metaphysic inspires but does not corrupt Lawrence's reporting; at its best superbly alive, it never falls into the fierce tedium and hysterical flouting of his worst abstractness.

THE PLUMED SERPENT

Few have agreed with Lawrence's own opinion—in any case quickly given up—that *The Plumed Serpent* was his best novel. It did what a novel could do, without totally collapsing, to feed his metaphysical fury and his fantasies of world decadence restored by sexual reformation and leadership. Narrative is pushed almost to the limit of self-absorbed prophetic sermonising; it survives, but by comparison with the work of the great period it is inelastic and deficient in its own kind of life.

Kate Leslie rejects her American friends; the book rejects White America in general as mechanical, tolerant, decadent, unable to perceive the 'reptile-like evil', the horror and squalor of a Mexico in the throes of a dreary revolution that is nothing but the imposition of white consciousness on blood consciousness. Mexico, for all its horrors, does not reverse Kate's life-flow as White Americans do. She falls in with a Spanish Mexican, Ramon, and an Indian, Cipriano, who are the founders of a cult of Quetzalcoatl, an ancient god who was replaced by the white Christ and will now return to succeed him. They celebrate the death of Christ and the new reign of the rejuvenated Quetzalcoatl, the Morning Star (for Lawrence found in the genuinely ancient cult of the planet Venus a symbol of that which reconciled

morning and night, an avatar of the Holy Ghost which re-
conciles absolute opposites). The gods are not indestruct-
ible, but the god-stuff is, taking new forms according to
human need. And modern Mexico needs not a saviour but
an authoritarian father; here the religion of *Kangaroo*
grows in more favourable soil. But the racial problem is
troublesome. 'Mexicans of mixed blood are hopeless,' says
one theorist (III). Yet throwing them out is hardly a solution, since after so long it's impossible to be sure that one
could distinguish 'pure-blooded Indians'. Must the country
remain in the hands of half-breeds, 'till the Americans …
flood in'? 'We shall be² as California and New Mexico now
are, swamped under the dead white sea.' Homogeneity of
blood alone ensures continuous consciousness; the pure-
blooded ensure it at the moment of coition. But now 'the
Indian consciousness is swamped under the stagnant water
of the white man's Dead Sea consciousness'. If there is any
hope it lies in the fostering of the ancient Indian consciousness, defeated and corrupt as it is.

Hence the new religion. Kate, like her maker, is both
ready for it and sceptical of it. She has Lawrence's *noli me
tangere*, later developed in the Lou of *St Mawr*, and finally
in *The Man Who Died*; she has his hatred of 'bottom-dogs'.
She combines with a desire to restart her broken life-flow an
unwillingness to join, and a readiness to ridicule and reject.
The war has taught her that the white race has lost its soul;
should she, knowing as Lawrence did that one can never
really go back, cluster round the drum? Lawrence knew he
couldn't; but Kate does. She is of course Irish, and so closer
to the Panic mystery (XI), though still not alien from the
world-destroying whites. She becomes involved in the mystery religion, though without entirely shedding her scepticism.

Quetzalcoatl, being the Morning Star, reconciler of cosmic male and female polarities, is the Holy Ghost. His coming is celebrated by rather chapel-like apocalyptic hymns as

well as dances to the drum, sermons and prose vedas. Lawrence works out the rituals for Ramon, an intellectual of a sort not unfamiliar in Europe, who takes up mythical revivalism and wants the Teutons to go back to Wotan, the Irish to Tuatha De Danaan (XVII). He prays from his lumbar ganglia while his devout Catholic wife, lamenting the frustration of the solar plexus, loves him like a mother and grieves over his apostasy from Jesus. Ramon celebrates the nowness of eternity, that fourth dimension in which shoot, root and blossom are one and each thing itself. The wife dies, like the old faith and the old style of marriage. But Kate moves towards Cipriano. She does not want to be touched, she desires fervently not to join the pantheon of a Mexican Salvation Army (XVII), but she wants even more to be saved from her fate as 'daughter of Eve, of greedy vision' (XII); and she marries Cipriano. The ceremony, later legalised, consists of invocations by Ramon in the pouring rain ('This man is my rain from heaven ... This woman is the earth to me' (XX)) during the period of the twilight of the Morning Star. She believes in the necessary small gulf between person and person (closing it is the sinful ambition of most women) and the need for each individual to be in touch directly with the cosmos; yet Cipriano's blood-knowledge draws her into 'the ancient phallic mystery' which, for women, is 'a mystery of prone submission ... submission absolute' (XX). She does become a goddess; she kills, and observes killing, without remorse. And although she has her sceptical moments ('they want to put it over me with their high-flown bunk' (XXII)), she cannot leave. Alone she is nothing: 'Only as the pure female corresponding to his pure male did she signify' (XXIV). She is to be a valley of blood complementary to his column of blood; and her satisfaction in this state of affairs is deeper than orgasm. Cipriano disapproves of female orgasm, which is frictional, 'the beak-like Aphrodite of the foam' (XXVI).

This denial of orgasm must appear to some to be the

apogee of the career of male chauvinism on which Lawrence embarked in the Preface of 1913. It is not altogether clear what he intended. Lady Chatterley has good orgasms, but also, before she meets Mellors, bad ones. She also learns to be content with none at all. The difference may well relate to some personal experience of a woman insisting on clitoral orgasm after the male ejaculation, a moment of *noli me tangere*. (Mabel Luhan oddly called Frieda 'the mother of orgasm' but not in a complimentary spirit, since in the same breath she called Lawrence 'a lively lamb tied to a solid stake', and plotted to remove that 'heavy, German hand' from his flesh (*N*. II. 167, 181).) What Kate is supposed to have learnt is an old Lawrentian lesson, that the ruin of Europe arises from the sexual demands of women, their ignorance of the truth that their fulfilment lies not in sexual satisfaction but in submission; whatever the real origin of Lawrence's equivocal rejection of female orgasm, it is represented as a rejection of trivial in favour of higher satisfactions. Sex with Cipriano is 'greater sex'. Kate doesn't take the whole Quetzalcoatl religion *au pied de la lettre*, but she does find in its prescriptions for marriage an explanation of her own needs: 'Rather than become elderly and a bit grisly, I will make my submission; as far as I need, and no further' (XXVII). She hears Ramon's last hymn, which celebrates the true union of men and women under the blessing of the Morning Star, in the tent of the Holy Ghost. It is an allegory of Lawrence's New Time, but also of personal rebirth, of one's submission to the law of the cosmos. Kate understands the nature of this religious fiction. At the end of the book we see her taking her leave, but Lawrence characteristically breaks off on a narrative ambiguity. She may turn round and go back. But there is nothing uncertain about her understanding.

The Quetzalcoatl religion has sometimes been dismissed as a piece of self-indulgence which spoils the book. Certainly it is often tiresome, over-developed; but it clearly has its place, being, in relation to the main purpose of the novel, much what Lawrence's mythological and psychological systems are to his fiction. The deliberate invention of a fictive religion must have been intended to clear that up. The battering such systems take from the play of sceptical (and often female) intelligence affects all his narratives, but none so clearly and diagrammatically as this one. Lawrence has, so to speak, internalised the metaphysical referent.

What weakens the book is not the inclusion of this fictive religion itself but the spurious rhetoric which attends it, and the unacceptable hieratic posturing of the narrative. Kate's scepticism is not well enough deployed to break up these poses. Still, the novel works better than *Kangaroo*, where Lawrence's insecurity forces him to taunt the reader, explain that he doesn't care what the reader thinks, that he can run along if he doesn't like it. It is worth noting that by the time this book came out understanding of Lawrence's strengths was well developed; the secure subtlety of his response to landscape, beasts, alien life-styles, was admired in spite of all that intervened to systematise them falsely, and the reviews of L. P. Hartley and Katherine Anne Porter prove that he had better readers in 1926 than he thought.[3] This makes it a little harder to understand the relative collapse of his reputation so soon afterwards; perhaps the scandals of the last years, the habit of reading memoirs which emphasised the peculiarity of the author rather than that of his work, and the increasing conformity of reality with his more offensive fantasies will go some way to explain it.

The Woman Who Rode Away, written between drafts of *The Plumed Serpent*, is sometimes considered as a partner to the novel. The woman escapes from an American marriage and rides off to seek Indians in barbarous Mexico. She finds them, and tells them despite their cruelty, indifference and unintelligibility, that she will give her heart to their god. They dress her in blue, the colour of the dead, and ritually kill her. It is often said that this story, with its powerful landscapes and its economy of notation, is better than *The Plumed Serpent*; and so in a sense it is, for in obvious ways brevity could save Lawrence. But it cannot achieve what requires length, namely internal criticism of the fiction, and this was also important to Lawrence. The end of the tale is naked doctrine, racial mastery.

ST MAWR

St Mawr is a focus of contention; it can be a leading document in the case against Lawrence as well as for him. It strikes me as one of the most achieved of his works. A woman's rejection of what passes for sex in the modern world, her acceptance of separateness and authentic contact with the cosmos—stated thus the theme sounds almost too familiar. But the book says much more. I think of it as the work which best shows how the insights of the Hawthorne essay were reflected in Lawrence's own writing.

The horse St Mawr has ancestors, notably in the dream described in *Fantasia* (199), in *The Boy in the Bush*, and in the apocalyptic animals of *The Rainbow*. Yet the figuration is new. Lou's marriage to Rico, the disoriented American woman to the Anglo-Australian hollow man, is also of a familiar type, the exhaustingly nervous, frictional, peaceless union. What distinguishes it is the density with which Rico's half-life as man and artist and friend is rendered; and his relationship with St Mawr, which is one of hatred between primitive male blood-knowledge and the highly strung parody of maleness that the man represents. The narrative shows how the different, brutal life of the horse—so insistently representative of 'another world', the non-human world of Pan—damages Rico and changes Lou's world to one of separateness in an inhuman landscape.

Most impressive is the doubling of narrative and symbolic senses. The grooms Phoenix and Lewis, Indian and Celt, are skilfully characterised but also bear heavy doctrinal charges. Even in the difficult scene when Lewis speaks of his beliefs, and argues with Lou's mother, Mrs Witt, about the meaning of the shooting star, one is not inclined to speak of self-indulgence, though the passage certainly relates to a new strain of apocalypticism that now obsesses Lawrence. Mrs Witt herself is presented in real depth —a demonstration of defensive worldly intelligence, a middle-aged woman defending herself with candour, irony and death-worship, against a world grown intolerably trivial. She has a doctrinal role, but it does not usurp personality. So with the New Mexican landscape of the conclusion; its metaphysical implications do not reduce its physical presence. It is the antithesis of England's countryside, which has grown 'little, old, unreal'—the American wilderness into which Lawrence, following so many admired New World authors, sends his heroine to find herself. The Pan whom they had merely discussed in Shropshire confronts them alive in New Mexico, as Lawrence observed in the essay 'Pan in America' (*P*. I. 22–31).

The sense of complex and hopeless corruption, out of which the doctrine is born, here takes precedence over the doctrine. Not that the book lacks doctrine. There is the usual racism; there are discussions of favourite themes—the overvaluation of intellect, the need to go beyond love, and 'evil, evil, evil, rolling in great waves over the earth ... a soft, subtle thing, soft as water ... a rapid return to the chaos' (79). Even St Mawr is part of this evil, though Rico is the worst part. It is the evil which will give fascism its chance. In this way the preaching and the narrative conspire with a kind of urgency to speak of the same thing. Everybody is part of the evil : Mrs Witt cutting Lewis's hair and, even while she loves him, unable to respect his separateness; the ultimate parasitic cheapness of Phoenix; the evil eye and rearing legs of St Mawr, tainted by the 'vulgar evil' (82) of men. Lou attributes to the stallion a despair at the ignobility of men which accounts for his abstention from the mares. But he recovers his sex in New Mexico, which is for her a place of therapeutic chastity and solitude.

Why does the woman need to renounce sex? In Shropshire the wife of the Dean, attributing the violence of St Mawr to 'evil male cruelty' (90), is making what for Lawrence was a characteristic mistake of degenerate womanhood and decadent Christianity : with a fine touch he compares the 'mean cruelty' of her humanitarianism with Rico's 'eunuch cruelty' (100). It is from all this that Lou escapes. *Noli me tangere*; she goes beyond the touch of men into that otherness from which the truth alone comes. 'Man and woman should stay apart, till they have learned to be gentle with one another again' (130). She leaves the 'arctic horror' (136) for the mountains of the south, alone—not as Birkin and Ursula left it, for Italy, together. She escapes from the 'friction' (147), leaving behind not only the rat-sexuality of Phoenix but even 'the illusion of the beautiful St Mawr' (147); she embraces a positive chastity, knowing better than to expect the 'mystic new man' (150).

The conclusion of *St Mawr* is one of Lawrence's most fully imagined pieces. The landscape is more splendid and awful than a man-god, a saviour; beautiful and brutal, it has horrors which are not those of civilisation and its 'Augean stables of metallic filth'. On a ranch subject to natural catastrophes—drought, packrats, disease—Lou passes beyond Law and Love, far beyond decadent sex sensation, choosing instead the wild America where 'a wild spirit wants me'. Her aspirations are questioned by her sceptical mother; but the mother is on the side of death, Lou on the more terrible side of life.

It is sometimes said that Lawrence got too much wrong : Rico's clothes, Lou's title, having St Mawr ridden in Hyde Park, where stallions are forbidden, not seeing, as English horsemen would, that Rico's accident was his own fault, or that no lady would have behaved as Mrs Witt did, startling the horse and endangering her son-in-law. Mr Hough uses a good many such arguments to support his point: Lawrence, returning disgusted from the visit to England which provided the Shropshire scenes of the story, was guilty of a falseness in putting a pasteboard England in competition with a beautiful wild America; Lou is not really doing anything there anyway, and the problems of civilisation, though real enough, are not to be solved in this way.[4] I do not feel the force of these difficulties, which seem at best trivial in the light of such a reading as that of Dr Leavis—surely the best study of any single Lawrence tale. *St Mawr* avoids the diagrammatic quality that spoils *The Princess* (frigid white woman cruelly treated by sexually vengeful Indian) and the sensationalism of *None of That*, a story written a year or two later, in which a rich American woman is raped by six of the assistants of a Mexican Indian bullfighter. Such a story is evidence of Lawrence's desperate situation; a sense of horror and of a world ending may distort as well as quicken the narrative imagination. He was entering another bad time; in February 1925 he had his almost fatal illness, and in the following autumn he left New Mexico for good.

Chapter Four   1925–1930

[*Lady Chatterley's Lover, The Man Who Died*]

After a short stay in England in October 1925 the Lawrences went via Germany to Italy. Apart from a few weeks
in the late summer of 1926 he never returned to a country
for whose inhabitants he felt increasing disgust. The Lawrences continued to wander, living in Majorca as well as in
Tuscany and Provence, though they settled for almost two
years in the Villa Mirenda near Florence. During these last
five years of his life Lawrence, though in worse and worse
health, remained prolific. His works included *Lady Chatterley's Lover*, many stories, including *The Virgin and the
Gipsy* and *The Man Who Died*, the travel book *Etruscan
Places*, some of his best poetry, including *Pansies*, and some
important non-fictional prose, including the essay on Galsworthy, the 'Introduction to these Paintings', *A Propos of
Lady Chatterley's Lover*, *Pornography and Obscenity*, and
the unfinished *Apocalypse*. He also painted some pictures
which got him into trouble with the police, provoked yet
again by the candour Lawrence found necessary to the expression of his latest insights into the nature of our needs.
Writing to his Buddhist friend Earl Brewster, he said he had
to 'put a phallus, a lingam you call it, in each of my pictures somewhere. And I paint no picture that won't shock
people's castrated social spirituality. I do this out of a positive belief, that the phallus is a great sacred image; it represents a deep, deep life which has been denied in us and still
is denied. Women deny it horribly, with a grinning travesty
of sex' (*C.L.* 967).

There was a change in the temper of Lawrence's thought;
although he still hankered after some kind of community
with a ritual basis (as his letters to Rolf Gardiner demon-

strate) he no longer saw himself as a leader, whether in a commune or a political party, which is what Gardiner would have liked (*N*. III. 474). In March 1928 he accepted Witter Bynner's criticism of the leadership mystique in *The Plumed Serpent*: 'On the whole, I think you're right. The hero is obsolete, and the leader of men is a back number ... the leader-cum-follower relationship is a bore. And the new relationship will be some sort of tenderness, sensitive, between men and women, and not the one up one down, lead on I follow, *ich dien* sort of business. So you see I'm becoming a lamb at last...' (*C.L.* 1045). It was in these years that he corresponded with the American psychoanalyst Trigant Burrow, whose emphasis on the societal basis of repression appealed to him much more strongly than Freudianism. But this did not affect the old association in Lawrence's mind between sexual and social decadence, nor, in the long run, his blaming women for it. 'One resents bitterly a certain swindle about modern life, and especially a sex swindle. One is swindled out of one's proper sex life, a great deal,' he says, in the same letter which complained of women's horrible denial of the phallus. Writing to Burrow, he offers a qualification of the old millennialism: 'There will *never* be a millennium. There will *never* be a "true societal flow"—all things are relative. Men were never, in the last, fully societal—and they never will be in the future. But more so, more than now. Now is the time between Good Friday and Easter. We're absolutely in the tomb' (*C.L.* 993). Despite the change in tone, the basic diagram of Lawrence's beliefs is unaltered. His apocalyptic interests grew stronger, and his disgust at the deadness of the world was considerably enhanced by the reception given to his advocacy of phallic tenderness.

Etruscan Places (1932) records Lawrence's 'instinctive' sympathy with the lost civilisation of Tuscany, crushed by Rome. He thought this civilisation, dominated by the emblems of phallus and womb, a deeper and more beautiful

culture than that of its conquerors. And in a sense it survives the conqueror : 'Italy today is far more Etruscan than
Roman ... The Etruscan element is like the grass of the field
and the sprouting of corn, in Italy : it will always be so.
Why try to revert to the Latin-Roman mechanism and suppression?' (II). This is a reference to the classic posturings of
Italian Fascism. Lawrence saw the Etruscan as he saw the
American Indian : his ancient blood-civilisation persisted,
and would be restored when the new time began; his
ancient religion was the original and universal religion,
celebrating the myriad vitalities of an organic cosmos.

In that hidden world there were initiates, who both knew
and felt, and the profane who merely felt, but were 'always
kept *in touch*, physically with the mysteries' (III). Lawrence
reads into Etruria the mystery religion, with its rites of
death and rebirth, its esoteric caste of initiates, that he was
also to discover, hidden under Jewish and Christian sophis-
tications, in the text of the Book of Revelation. In the pre-
Apollonian world of this religion there was true sensual
knowledge, an authentic delight in, and on proper occasions
horror of, life, the phallic mystery.

There are passages in *Etruscan Places* which are alive
with intelligence and poetry—for example, the treatment
of augury and astrology, or the descriptions of tomb-paint-
ing, no less precise in themselves because they must bear
the weight of Lawrence's primeval theology. He dreams of
an aristocratic and phallic tenderness which is nevertheless
capable of being cruelly in tune with the life-mystery; he
cultivates a sense of that mystery which contains an
ancient ambiguity, being sacred to the initiate, and obscene
to the profane. It is not surprising that in his own imaginative work of this period Lawrence tried to reproduce this
mystery, and with similar consequences.

The myth of aristocratic, secret-sacred knowledge, earlier
associated with the American Indians, is now figured forth
by the ancient mystery religion, universal in a pre-glacial,

prelapsarian world, a world before the collapse into mentalism. Lawrence was not the first thinker to invent a history in order to justify a metaphysic or an aesthetic; and such inventions have in common a conviction that only some aboriginal catastrophe can explain the degree of our decadence, the fervour of our hopes for renovation. What distinguishes Lawrence's myth is the degree to which it can build on older layers of apocalypticism in his thought.

As we have seen, the war made passionate and immediate an apocalyptic interest as old as his experience of chapel hymns. During the war he read works on occult symbolism and theosophy. The idea that Revelation is a distorted account of a Greek mystery religion is present in the work of Mme Blavatsky; whether or no he got it there, Lawrence, in January 1916, asked Lady Ottoline Morrell to send him the Homeric Hymns in connection with his reading in primitive anthropology and 'Orphic religions' (*C.L.* 416). (The 'Hymn to Demeter' is an important source of information on the Eleusinian Mysteries.) Later he did some quite intensive reading in apocalyptic scholarship both orthodox and unorthodox, showing some contempt for the former. And about the time of *St Mawr* he fell in with Frederick Carter, an occultist who was writing a work entitled *The Dragon of the Apocalypse*. He read 'Carter's first draft in Mexico, speaking of the sense of release it gave him to move out of astronomy into astrology; 'the Macrocosm, the great sky with its meaningful stars' (*P.* I. 293), and near the end of his life wrote a Preface for Carter's book; a much longer introduction which he had to put aside was published posthumously as the unfinished *Apocalypse*. Carter had meanwhile come to think his original manuscript unsound. 'But who cares?' asks Lawrence. 'We do not care, vitally, about theories of the Apocalypse: what the Apocalypse means. What we care about is the release of the imagination ... What does the Apocalypse matter, unless in so far as it gives us imaginative release into another vital world?' (*P*. I. 294).

This is a characteristic disclaimer, and should be remembered whenever one is discussing the metaphysic of Lawrence. He makes the point finely in *Etruscan Places*. It does not mean that he thought any nonsense would serve provided that it led one to a kind of ecstatic sense of the cosmos, nor does it mean that the intelligence is not to be engaged. He tries to be truthful and accurate in writing about Revelation, exactly as the augurs did when reading entrails. But truth and accuracy would seem dead indeed if unrelated to imaginative release. I do not mean that Lawrence never talked nonsense, and that the metaphysic did not many times prevail over invention, the teller over the tale. But we shall never get him right if we simply treat these speculations as irresponsible loose-mouthed foolery.

So, in *Apocalypse*, which is the key metaphysical work of this final period, he develops with some enthusiasm what is essentially a scholarly hypothesis : that the extant text of St John's Revelation contains, under its allegories, the symbols of true universal religion 'plastered over' by later dogmatic accretions, and untranslatable into Apollonian discursive terms (he follows Nietzsche in regarding Socrates as the destroyer of the old Dionysian world). He accepted Carter's argument that Revelation has astrological significance, and approved of this, since it was a way of avoiding the way of our 'living death' (*P*. I. 299), which substitutes balls of gas and stone for the living creatures called sun and moon; but the Apocalypse is not merely starmyth; it is also 'a revelation of Initiation experience' (*C.L.* 744–5). And he continued the enquiry which should uncover this experience under 'the all-too-moral chapel meaning of the book' (*P*. I. 302). Carter, in his book on Lawrence (*D. H. Lawrence and the Body Mystical*, 1932) thinks Lawrence got some of his arguments wrong, but Lawrence would not have thought this important.

According to Lawrence, the Book of Revelation as we have it is corrupted by Jewish and Christian morality. Its origin is in mystery-religion, but the written account is corrupted first by Jewish and then by Christian revisions. The present text results from an attempt on the part of underdogs to be revenged on the elect; the truth is garbled by the ugly power-lust of the second-rate. Hence the powerful appeal of Revelation, through the ages, to the second-rate, the underdog. Christian renunciation will not serve for most men—it is an aristocratic ideal; so Revelation, in its biblical form, gives 'the death kiss to the Gospels' (III). It successfully encourages the neglect of Christ as cosmocrator, as Hermes, Lord of Heaven and Hell, in favour of the 'petty personal adventure' (V) of modern Christianity.

This rediscovery of the ur-Revelation is a way of relearning the old lesson of the vital correspondence between our lives and that of the cosmos, a necessary lesson in these times which witness 'the long, slow death of the human being' (VI) in a world of science and machinery. Reading it correctly, penetrating the layers of sophistication, we discover that Revelation has a first section that is optimistic and renovatory, and a second which reflects 'simple lust for the end of the world' (VI). (How well Lawrence knew these feelings could coexist in one book!) But behind the text of John, 'the power-worshipping Jew' (VI) we can find the mystery which is the key to pagan consciousness. There are seven cycles, related to the body of man, and to his seven spheres of consciousness. The four horses (man lost the horse in the epoch when he lost himself) stand for the four humours, and for the reduction of the body; the pale horse is 'the little death' suffered by the initiate. And so through the symbols of rebirth, till there remains only 'a new whole cloven flame of a new-bodied man with golden thighs and a face of glory' (X); at the opening of the seventh seal the mystic initiate is twice-born, and there is silence in heaven.

At this point the ur-text ends. The rest of the Book has

the Trumpets to parallel the Seals, two Witnesses signifying the twin powers of blood and water, united in the phallus, and also signifying our dual consciousness. The Woman Clothed with the Sun is Magna Mater, split into two (the other half being the Whore) by Jewish meddling. So with the Dragon, of which only the malefic aspect is presented. Originally, in the Christian interpretation, it was the Logos; now it is that mad form of consciousness which entraps us, and especially woman. Remembering the rituals of Quetzalcoatl, Lawrence argues for a primitive threefold cosmos, sun, moon and morningstar, the reconciler; add four, which is the number of creation, and you have the magical seven; for magic, like astrology, is a decadent survivor of the old consciousness. But such interpretations are obscured by the mechanised, scientific world. In his final pages Lawrence considers the implications for modern communal life of our alienation from these primitive truths. We live under the curse of democracy and power-seeking, which supplant the dark consciousness of the universe originally possessed by men. We have lost *connection*—'with the cosmos, with the world, with mankind, with the nation, with the family ... That is our malady' (XXIII). The true Apocalypse shows us our place in 'the magnificent here and now of life ... We ought to dance with rapture that we should be alive and in the flesh, and part of the living, incarnate cosmos ... There is nothing of me that is alone and absolute except my mind, and we shall find that the mind has no existence by itself, it is only the glitter of the sun on the surface of the waters' (XXIII).

The fact that *Apocalypse* is about the least read of Lawrence's works explains many errors of interpretation. The machinery of it doesn't matter in itself, only as an illustration of how intellect contributed to the discoveries of Lawrence's imagination. Written very late, it handled themes that had occupied him for years. In 1923 he had a different interpretation for the seals and the vials (relating the first to the sympathetic, the second to the lumbar ganglia). It doesn't matter; what matters, as he always insisted, was the release of the imagination. A measure of the degree to which these speculations released his own imagination is his last novel. *Lady Chatterley's Lover* is closely associated with the late apocalyptic phase of Lawrence's thinking, to which it stands in the same relation as *Women in Love* to *The Crown*. I shall consider only the final version, finished in January 1928.[1]

LADY CHATTERLEY'S LOVER

Writing to Koteliansky when he was half way through the book, Lawrence called it 'the most improper novel ever written' (*C. L.* 1028), but denied that it was pornography. 'It's a declaration of the phallic reality.' He knew no English printer would handle it, and arranged for a private edition to be printed and published in Florence, 'the full fine flower with pistil and stamens standing'. He talked a great deal about this reassertion of the phallic as against 'cerebral sex-consciousness' (*C.L.* 1047), asserting that, while 'nothing nauseates me more than promiscuous sex', he wanted, in this novel, 'to make an *adjustment in consciousness* to the basic physical realities' (*C.L.* 1111). His attitude, as he admitted, was Puritan; he respected natural impulses but hated 'that pathological condition when the *mind* is absorbed in sex ... It is true that Lawrence himself was possessed by the subject of sex—but in what a different way! His possession was like that of a doctor who wishes to heal' (Earl Brewster, *N*. III. 135). He was perfectly aware of the trouble he would bring on himself by this last effort 'to make the sex relation valid and precious instead of shameful' (*C.L.* 972). There is no doubt that Lawrence, although he was later to be ill with bitterness against his countrymen for their response to this and other late works, intended to shock; that was part of the therapy.

He wanted to call the book *John Thomas and Lady Jane*, though sometimes he preferred *Tenderness*. Tenderness, as he explained to Bynner in a letter already quoted, was to replace leadership as the quality most necessary to the health of the world. But first it was necessary to purge the very lexicon of sex. The four-letter words which were still occupying so much attention at the trial of 1960 were obscene, he argued, only because of 'unclean mental associations': the important task, then, was to 'cleanse the mind' to end the associations of fear and dirt, to get rid of the tabu on such words. 'The kangaroo is a harmless animal, the word shit is a harmless word. Make either into a taboo, and it becomes most dangerous. The result of taboo is insanity. And insanity, especially mob-insanity, mass-insanity, is the fearful danger that threatens our civilisation ... If the young do not watch out, they will find themselves, before so many years are past, engulfed in a howling manifestation of mob-insanity, truly terrifying to think of. It will be better to be dead than to live to see it.'[2]

The change in consciousness which would make *Lady Chatterley's Lover* acceptable as 'tenderness' rather than 'obscenity' is one that the book itself desperately advocates, though at the same time taking it to be impossible without the intervention of the 'bad time' that it announces as on the way. It seems certain that the changes of consciousness which have in fact occurred to allow the free publication of the book are not of a kind that Lawrence would have approved; I expect he would have campaigned against the unrestricted use of such words as *fuck* in books and conversation. They can hardly be said to have acquired a tender, let alone a numinous quality; acceptable in common use, whether as expletives or as part of a genuinely sexual language, they have no doubt also been restored to the bourgeois bedroom; but they remain part of sex-in-the-head, or as instruments of the wrong kind of letting-go, which Lawrence detested equally, as a betrayal of the self. Hence Mellors's use of them, though it may impress liberal bishops, strikes most people as a bit comic, doctrinaire almost—at best the language of a lost paradise.

It may be that the whole attempt was misguided. The need, as Lawrence saw it, was to avoid euphemisms which are in themselves evidence of the sell-out of the passional to the intellectual; to restore the words which belong to the old blood-consciousness. But in so far as these words were secret and sacred they had value as ritual profanities; and so they became a part of the culture, proper to the expansive movements of constricted lives—a fact reflected in the heavy use made of them by soldiers and sailors, poor men in circumstances of sexual privation. Perhaps a good society would use them only with great semantic purity; but the history of our society, as Lawrence knew, and the history of the words also, were such that a lexical could not induce a spiritual purgation. Lawrence must, as he wrote and rewrote his story, have been partly conscious of this. The vile press reaction to the book, as represented by the hysteria of his old enemy *John Bull*, cannot have surprised him; nor, I suspect, would the knowledge that for thirty years after publication this innocent work was converted, by the minds of furtive purchasers, into precisely the pornography that he so abhorred. More recently we have come, now that it has sold its paperback millions, to find it tame, a reaction which would certainly have shocked him just as much.

Lady Chatterley's Lover is about the need for a rebirth of phallic consciousness conceived, in a familiar Lawrentian way, as the only means to regeneration both personal and national. The approaching death of the English, which he had prophesied in the war years, was an aspect of the final extinction of that old consciousness. The war had announced the Last Days, the bad time that would come, whether or no there was a rebirth. Constance Chatterley, like Ursula at moments, becomes, in part, a representation of England as a sleeping beauty, only to be revived by the *gros baiser* of a phallic prince. Always apocalyptic when he wrote of regeneration, Lawrence made this prophetic novel absorb much of the last version of his apocalyptic theory.

There is the sexuality of death—the impotence of Chatterley, the 'loving' of Michaelis—and there is something else, so far beyond it that the word *sex* barely applies to it, which is why, when he thought of Mellors, Lawrence habitually spoke not of sex but of the phallus as beyond sex. The sense of sexual experience as something to be passed through, as the prelude or initiation into a more satisfactory condition of life on the other side, is strong in him; so are the ideas of renunciation and chastity. A man who admits to having been in his youth enraged by the idea of a woman's sexuality ('I only wanted to be aware of her personality, her mind and spirit' (P. II. 568)) might well feel that the only good chastity must come after the restoration of the 'natural life-flow'. It is a further charge against the mother, that a son should regard sex as an improper secret; Lawrence's mother thought it indecent that there should be a seduction in *The White Peacock*: 'To think that *my* son should have written such a story' (N. I. 62). *Lady Chatterley's Lover* retains traces of the puritanism inherited from the mother, as well as evidence of a desire to take a last revenge on her, and on all the women who have ruined England; to them Connie will be the Scarlet Woman, to him she is the Woman Clothed with the Sun; St John took them apart, and Lawrence puts them together again as an emblem of a virtually impossible restoration.

Although Chatterley regards sex as an atavistic organic process (I) his impotence is a direct result of the war. The second sentence of the book places the story firmly in the post-war era: 'The cataclysm has happened, we are among the ruins' (I). It is a world of death and impotence; the melancholy park, the ruined countryside, the unmanned colliers, Chatterley in his mechanical chair. This is the background against which Connie's rebirth will be described. In the old world of death women use sex as an instrument by means of which to gain power over men. We recall that Kate, in *The Plumed Serpent*, had to forego orgasm; Lawrence seemed to think that a woman, holding back orgasm until after her partner's ejaculation, was merely asserting herself, preferring the quasi-masturbatory pleasure of clitoral orgasm induced by pelvic friction to unassertive submission or vaginal orgasm. In the end even the patient and skilful womaniser Michaelis, who let Connie get her satisfaction in this way, condemns her for it ('You couldn't go off at the same time as a man, could you? You'd have to bring yourself off! You'd have to run the show!' (IV); and full vaginal orgasm is a stage along the way to life in the affair with Mellors. 'Beaked' sex (clitoral orgasm) belongs in a world out of order; it is not distinct from the blighted countryside, from the ruined miners and their wives, who have lost even the sense of subordination, or from the lifeless, nervous stories of Chatterley.

The marriage of the Chatterleys is, of course, a sexless relationship quite unlike the positive chastity of Connie and Mellors at the close; far from being 'valid and precious' it is simply death. Connie's affair with Michaelis is another aspect of the profound degeneracy that Lawrence nearly always associated with race; Michaelis is Irish, but he has the look of 'a carved ivory Negro mask ... Aeons of acquiescence in race destiny, instead of our individual resistance. And then a swimming through, like rats in a dark river' (III). This is the Lawrentian imagery of degenerate corruption, *fin du race*; he returns to it, finding in Michaelis 'that ancient motionlessness of a race that can't be disillusioned any more, an extreme, perhaps, of impurity that is pure. On the far side of his supreme prostitution to the bitch-goddess he seemed pure, pure as an African ivory mask that dreams impurity into purity ...' (V). He stands for the fascinating racial corruption of the Last Days. And at this point the only voice that speaks of the need for a deeper blood-consciousness, a transformation of sex, is the somewhat implausible voice of Dukes ('Real knowledge comes out of the whole corpus of the consciousness; out of your belly and your penis as much as out of your brain and mind ... once you start the mental life you pluck the apple' (IV)). He gives a potted account of Lawrence's own views on this Fall, and extends it to cover the whole world-crisis; but set down as conversation with the sceptical Chatterley it is all thin and unconvincing; deliberately so, for we are to learn under a more gifted teacher.

The gamekeeper looks back to Annable in *The White Peacock*; the educated gamekeeper who has dropped out of civilisation into what is left of the natural world, that 'greenwood' into which E. M. Forster in *Maurice* dispatches his bourgeois drop-out with another gamekeeper. He is related to Lawrence's Indians and gipsies (*The Virgin and the Gipsy* was written only a short time before the novel), but the difference is important; he has found his way *out* of the white consciousness. This is why Lawrence makes him an educated man and an ex-officer, and why he gives him two dialects, middle-class and peasant. To the latter belong the famous four-letter words; spoken in the Chatterley dining-room they are nasty, here they are 'part of the natural flow' (P. II. 570). Mellors is also part of that flow; we see that when he pushes Chatterley's mechanical chair as well as when he goes about his gamekeeper's business; we see it in his difference from his social superiors. He inhabits his world alone and chaste; when he has to move into Connie's worn-out world he feels the 'bruise of the war' (V) but dreads rebirth; for that is what his relation with her must involve. As for Connie, she has to abandon the impurity of Michaelis, whose way is only down and out, for the way of Mellors, which is a passage through the gates of life and death (*Etruscan Places*, which also celebrates this mystical journey, is contemporary with the novel).

Mellors might have been a lay figure, representing Lawrentian opinions; he calls his little daughter a 'false little bitch' for crying dishonestly (VI) and holds the right views about marriage. In many ways he differs little from Dukes, with his prophesying of the end : 'Our old show will come flop; our civilisation is going to fall. It's going down to the bottomless pit, down the chasm. And believe me, the only bridge across the chasm will be the phallus' (VII). But Connie, though moved by this talk of 'the resurrection of the body' and a 'democracy of touch' (VII) finds more than words in Mellors; even as she deeply senses 'the end of all things' she is capable of receiving 'in her womb' the shock of the vision of the gamekeeper's body as he washed : 'the pure, delicate, white loins, the bones showing a little, and the sense of aloneness' (VI). She goes to him not in frustrated desire but in the need to be reborn in the last days—a harsh ecstasy, unlike that of Chatterley's surrender of his solar plexus (no stimulus possible to *his* lumbar ganglia) to Mrs Bolton.

What follows is her initiation and mystic rebirth, as in the original plot of Apocalypse; and Lawrence is suggesting that the novel itself mimes this process, for 'it can inform and lead into new places the flow of our sympathetic consciousness, and it can lead our sympathy away in recoil from things gone dead ... The novel, properly handled, can reveal the most secret places of life : for it is in the *passional* secret places of life, above all, that the tide of sensitive awareness needs to ebb and flow, cleansing and freshening (IX). Thus the novel fleshes out the scheme provided by the metaphysic. Lawrence, for example, knows better than to make Mrs Bolton a caricature or diagram, or neglect the broader social context. There must be flow and recoil, density. The newborn chick is a natural object, though Connie sees it 'eyeing the Cosmos' (X), and her crying at the sight is the recognisable reaction of a sensitive woman as well as the sign of 'her generation's forlornness' (X).

When they first make love Connie is content without orgasm. It is enough that in the mechanised, frictional world, rebirth may be on the way. Later, Lawrence has to try to find a prose capable of representing genuine orgasm; and later still Connie, after a few backslidings, a few profanations, must move into the next stage of passional knowledge, an awareness of the phallic mystery which includes a proper awe of man. Meanwhile the world seems even more horrible in its irrelevant excesses, its dissociation from the authenticities of the bloodstream; but Connie goes on with her initiation and is 'born: a woman' (XII). Remembering *Women in Love* once more, Lawrence allows her to say that 'it was the sons of god with the daughters of men'. Her dread of maleness is all but overcome; though Connie still can't quite break herself of the habit of talking about love, that alienating irrelevance. Life has returned; but the process is not complete.

The book represents Connie's initiation into mystery as having seven stages, like the seven stages in the mystery-religion behind Revelation. She progressively comes alive; she can dance in the unspoiled part of the wood, and tell her husband that the body, killed by Plato and Jesus, will be reborn: 'it will be a lovely, lovely life in the lovely universe, the life of the human body' (XVI) she says, echoing the Lawrentian view that eternity is a fourth-dimensional apprehension of the life of the body here and now. 'My dear, you speak as if you were ushering it all in!' says Chatterley. But there remains an ultimate stage of purgation, the sensuality which is 'necessary ... to burn out the false shames and smelt out the heaviest ore of the body into purity'—the exploration by the phallus of 'the last and deepest recesses of organic shame' (XVI). They must go beyond tenderness, though when the experience is over Connie begs Mellors not to forget tenderness for ever.

Chapter XVI of *Lady Chatterley's Lover* contains what has become the most controversial passage in all of Lawrence's novels. The fact that it describes anal intercourse was long ignored; nobody mentioned it at the 1960 trial. The question has now been argued at length,[3] and the discussion need not be repeated here. As in *Women in Love*, the climactic sexual act is an act of buggery, conceived as a burning out of shame. The invasion of the genital by the excremental, the contamination of joy by shame and life by death, was a strategy for the overthrow of the last enemy. We have seen that Lawrence had earlier thought of these polarities as reconcilable only by a third force, his Holy Ghost; the phallus, its representative, will bridge the flows of dissolution and creation, which, coming together in the genitalia, also come together in history, at this moment. The metaphysic is very complicated, not least because Lawrence is less candid at such moments than in describing more ordinary sexual activity; but he is again fighting the woman-inspired *pudeur* which has blanched sex-consciousness, made women 'fribbles' and emasculated men.

In *Women in Love* he tried to distinguish between buggery which was wholly dissolute and buggery that was initiatory, the symbolic death before rebirth, the cracking of the insect carapace. Culturally, the parallel is this : we have to get to the point where nothing is left of our mistaken civilisation, and the Holy Ghost can institute the third Joachite epoch. The forbidden acts of Gerald and Gudrun, or Birkin and Hermione, or Mellors and Bertha, are merely corruption within the rind; the same acts committed by Birkin and Ursula, Connie and Mellors, are the acts of healthy human beings. When 'no dark shameful things are denied her' Ursula is 'free' (*W. in L.* XXX). The next step for Gudrun is death. For Connie it is a ritual death, with the phallus as psychopomp. She experiences what is 'necessary, forever necessary, to burn out false shames' (XVI). No need ever to do it again; now there can be tenderness, and even chastity.

This is the climatic sexual encounter, for the last, described in XVIII, is a kind of marital epilogue and belongs to initiated tenderness, not to the harsh initiatory experience we are talking about. To Chatterley Mellors's reputation (there was talk of his buggering his wife) was merely an illustration of man's 'strange avidity for unusual sexual postures' (XVII); but Lawrence wasn't as a rule of Chatterley's opinion, and clearly does not want us to be.

This was a bold thing to have done, and obviously it was a matter of importance to Lawrence. One thinks of Milton's necessary audacity in describing the lovemaking of the angels; each writer, we may think, could well have avoided the course he follows. But Milton could not think his interpenetrating angels redundant; they were of the stuff of his imagination. Lawrence was equally committed to this reconciliation of dissolution and creation in anal sex. Mellors, in the England of Lloyd George, is the Saint George who kills the dragon (the serpent of corruption, of shame at defecation) and sets the lady free; an act as apocalyptic as that of Spenser's St George. And he also opened her seven seals to initiate her. In the end, as Lawrence said of Chatterley's paralysis, 'Whether we call it symbolism or not, it is, in the sense of its happening, inevitable' (*P.* II. 514). What made it so was the force of Lawrence's belief in the phallus as the Comforter, the reconciler, the agent of rebirth. And just as Lawrence himself recognised, when he read his first draft, that Chatterley's lameness symbolised 'the paralysis, the deeper emotional or passional paralysis, of most men of his sort and class today' (*P.* II. 514) so we recognise the symbolism of Connie's rebirth. Both symbolisms belong to a metaphysic which Lawrence had long since internalised, and which the tale had, in its own way, to make objective. If we trust them it is because we trust the tale.

Lady Chatterley's Lover, like most of Lawrence's novels, has astonishing lapses; he occasionally allows himself risqué sexual punning which, in this context, obviously constitutes a dangerous mistake; and occasionally he lapses into the jeering viciousness of some of the work of the preceding years. But it remains a great achievement, not only in itself but in the change it helped to bring about in Lawrence himself. The book ends on a 'long pause', the pause between epochs. Lawrence filled the pause in his own life with poems, pictures, one of the greatest of his stories (which is also about rebirth into creativity) and some of his most impressive and enduring polemical-discursive prose.

PORNOGRAPHY AND OBSCENITY

By this last I mean the essays *A Propos of Lady Chatterley's Lover*, *Pornography and Obscenity*, and a few related pieces.[4] Lawrence had fought bruising battles with various censors before, and he must have known his later work would run into trouble, especially when the oppressive Joynson-Hicks was Home Secretary. *A Propos of Lady Chatterley's Lover*, an expansion of *My Skirmish with Jolly Roger* (1929) was published in the last year of Lawrence's life. Its importance is that Lawrence must here, in the process of justifying his unconventional novel, express his sense of cultural and sexual crisis, and his recommendations as to conduct, with little aid from myth or metaphysic. His 'honest, healthy book' (P. II. 489)—so he describes *Lady Chatterley*—is a contribution to that evolved culture in which tabu and superstition, obscurity and violence, will have been eliminated from our thinking about sex. Not, he says, that we should necessarily increase sexual activity; but there must be clear thinking about it, even by those whose role is to abstain. And this calls for improvements in sexual education, for the benefit not only of those tragically ignorant of sex, but also of 'the advanced young' who 'go to the other extreme and treat it as a sort of toy to be played with, a slightly nasty toy' (491). The 'perversion of smart licentiousness' is no better than 'the perversion of puritanism' (492). We live in a world of fake sexual emotion; only true sex can change it. 'When a "serious" young man said to me the other day : "I can't believe in the regeneration of England by sex, you know," I could only say, "I'm sure you can't." He had no sex anyhow ... And he didn't know what it meant, to have any' (496). To such young people sex is at best the 'trimmings', thrills and fumbling. Real sex seems to them barbaric.

Lawrence believes in fidelity as essential to good sex, and therefore in indissoluble marriage; the sacramentality of marriage is the greatest boon of the Church, a recognition of a balance and a rhythm which is reflected in the liturgy and binds sex to the seasons. But the marriage has to be phallic, the column of blood in the valley of blood, the remaking of paradise. It is not to be a union of 'personalities', a nervous indulgence, 'frictional and destructive' (507). Such sex will certainly not regenerate England. What is required is not a *logos*, a Word, but rather a Deed, 'the *Deed* of life' (510). Only thus may we be restored to a healthy relation with the cosmos. Buddha, Plato, Jesus, cut us off from life; we have to get back to ancient forms, Apollo, Attis, Demeter, Persephone; to the threefold relationship of man and universe, man and woman, man and man. The isolation of 'personality'—typified by Clifford Chatterley— 'the death of the great humanity of the world' (513)—is what must end; the restoration of a phallic language was the means chosen in Lawrence's last novel to bring this about.

That a revolution in the passional lives of men and women must precede the establishment of the good society; and that this change, though in one sense revolutionary, will require a return to mythic origins, to the human condition that prevailed before some aboriginal catastrophe, is not doctrine peculiar to Lawrence. An obvious ancestor, among others, is Nietzsche; but such notions were in the air. The 'dissociation of sensibility', to use Eliot's term, is an old doctrine, and Lawrence knew it very early, perhaps as early as 1906, if that was the year in which he told Jessie Chambers that there could never be another Shakespeare, for Shakespeare was the product of an integrated age, whereas 'things are split up now'.[5] Early in 1929 he wrote an introduction to a projected book on his paintings, and in this extraordinary essay he found occasion to examine the nature of the dissociation in more historical detail. The reason why the English can't paint is fear, fear of life; and Lawrence, now arguing that this fear is already visible in Shakespeare, dates it from the Renaissance, and specifically from the syphilis epidemic of the sixteenth century. 'The grand rupture had started in the human consciousness' (*P. I.* 552). The division between mental and physical consciousness was established; sex was associated with terror, and intuitive awareness of other people, and of nature, was lost. The art of the eighteenth century is optical rather than intuitive, the body disappears from painting; even the French Impressionists escaped into light. The chaos of modernism begins in this terror. Lawrence is particularly hard on Significant Form, a Bloomsbury doctrine. What he recounts 'is the nauseating and repulsive history of the crucifixion of the procreative body for the glorification of the spirit, the mental consciousness ... The Renaissance put the spear through the side of the already crucified body, and syphilis put poison into the wound made by the imaginative spear ... We were born corpses' (569). Cézanne moved the stone from the door of the tomb, but the critics rolled it back; and English artists have reached a condition of death, whether or no this is a prelude to rebirth.

Here we have a new historical version of Lawrence's myth of the lost paradise, of the forfeited blood-consciousness and the closed imaginative eye. Such myths are normally inspired by a strong sense of the desperate needs of one's own epoch, and Lawrence's is certainly no exception to the rule. He wrote *Lady Chatterley* and *A Propos* as contributions to an urgently needed passional revolution. His metaphysic grew increasingly conscious of practical needs of the moment; hence the restored sexual vocabulary, and hence a further attempt to justify it in the pamphlet *Pornography and Obscenity*, published in the same series as one by Joynson-Hicks which stated the opposing case.

Of all Lawrence's writings this is the work that has kept best as a contribution to a continuing debate. It states the need for true sex in art, and the rightness of genuine sexual stimulus; Boccaccio seems to him less pornographic than *Jayne Eyre* or *Tristan und Isolde*. True pornography, however, ought to be censored; it is what does dirt on sex. And here Lawrence tames and uses an old theory of his: 'The sex functions and the excrementory functions in the human body work so close together, yet they are, so to speak, utterly different in direction. Sex is a creative flow, the excrementory flow is towards dissolution, decreation ... In the really healthy human being the distinction between the two is instant ... But in the degraded human being the deep instincts have gone dead, and then the two flows become identical. *This* is the secret of really vulgar and pornographical people: the sex flow and the excrement flow is the same thing to them. It happens when the psyche deteriorates, and the profound controlling instincts collapse. Then sex is dirt and dirt is sex, and sexual excitement becomes a playing with dirt' (*P.I.* 176).

The clarity of this insight will survive the criticism that it does nothing to aid a censor's choice between the creative and the excrementatory in literary sex, much less enable unqualified lawyers and juries to make it. Its survival is a function of its utter seriousness, its dedication to the idea that life must be kept up, that sex is not a 'dirty little secret' though it can be made so by pornographers and magistrates alike. Thus the abstractions of the metaphysic prove to be rooted in life; and this is what people mean when they declare that Lawrence was always, whatever he might seem to be doing, a most moral writer.

His disgust at pornography depends in a measure upon his hatred of masturbation, a practical way of turning a procreative into an excrementatory function. Masturbation is another consequence of the lies we tell about sex; to be free of the lies would mean to be free not only of masturbation but of the lies that 'lurk under the cloak of this one primary lie', for example 'the monstrous lie of money ... Kill the purity lie, and the money lie will be defenceless' (185). So once again sexual reform is the key to cultural and economic reform. Lawrence here has the consistency that a fully-developed metaphysic affords. And as usual in the midst of death he finds some hope of rebirth; there is a minority, he ends, which 'hates the lie ... and which has its own dynamic ideas about pornography and obscenity' (186–7). One may doubt that the achievement of that minority—the Obscenity Act of 1959 and its successors, the successful defence of *Lady Chatterley's Lover* but also of other books which Lawrence would probably have wanted to censor—would have gratified him. But this is part of the general truth that the revolution which has occurred in our handling of the 'dirty little secret' is hardly at all the revolution Lawrence wanted. Our literary sex, like the pill and the modern commune, would have had him once more prophesying the last days and the need for rebirth. He always thought of the movies as a masturbatory medium; he castigated them in *The Lost Girl*, in the late poem 'When I went to the Film', in which the audience is 'moaning from close-up kisses, black-and-white kisses that could not be felt'[6] and in *Pornography and Obscenity*. It is not conceivable that the coloured sex of our cinema would have pleased him more. The reason why he is so often called a puritan is that he thought that sex was the key to life and spiritual regeneration, and also that these were solemn matters.

THE MAN WHO DIED

Lawrence's last long story was *The Man Who Died*, a parable of rebirth. First called *The Escaped Cock*, and written in two parts in 1927 and 1928, in a new finely sustained hieratic tone, it is one of the most perfect of Lawrence's shorter fictions. A peasant's cock escapes its leash; Jesus awakes in the tomb. Lawrence's *noli me tangere* now returns to its source; the reborn Jesus, 'beyond loneliness', returning to the life of nature after the disillusion of death. He captures the cock and lodges with the peasant. The cock, and the colours and vitality of the spring landscape, persuade him of the 'surge of life'. He encounters Mary Magdalene ('Don't touch me, Madeleine') and tells her that his mission is over, that his business is now his 'own, single life'. He remembers his own past complicity in treachery and egotism, and looks forward only to meeting a woman 'who can lure my risen body, yet leave me my aloneness', the aloneness of the cock he has carried with him. Meanwhile he preserves himself from the touch of others, the egotists, fearers of death. In the second part of the tale he meets a priestess of Isis, whose task it is to seek the fragments of the dead Osiris, her reborn husband. Thus 'the man who had died and the woman of the pure search' come together; 'I have risen naked and branded. But if I am naked enough for this contact, I have not died in vain. Before I was clogged.' At last he rises into life, and is ready again to touch and be touched. When the priestess has conceived he withdraws: 'I have sowed the seed of my life and my resurrection.'

This remarkable parable is the best demonstration of a belief always held by Lawrence, and a good belief for a writer: that rebirth is into this life, and that eternity is the fullness of this life—what he sometimes called its fourth dimension. A man achieves it by avoiding commonplace touching, by dying and rising separate, and then achieving union with 'the woman of the pure search'. The situation of Jesus partly resembles the gamekeeper in the novel; the flame that Mellors speaks of, coming into being between him and Connie, is, in his own word, 'Pentecostal', and it is from such unions alone—Jesus and the Isis-girl, Mellors and Connie—that Lawrence's Holy Ghost and his Joachite Third Epoch will take its rise. He was never surer of what he was, and of what he needed to do, than in these last difficult years. The poetry of *Pansies*, even the cocksureness of *Nettles* and the condemnatory essay on Galsworthy, are all of a piece with the late works here discussed.

Lawrence was dying. What he thought of death he put into *The Man Who Died* and into such poems as 'Bavarian Gentians' and 'The Ship of Death'.

> *All that matters is to be at one with the living God*
> *to be a creature in the house of the God of Life.*[6]

The passage of oblivion which the dead must take, and the untouched apartness of that death-in-life which is the preparation for rebirth, come together. *The Man Who Died* is an assertion of life in death; so is the work of Lawrence as a whole, which is why people like to say, inadequately, that even if he was on the side of many things they dislike he was also on the side of life, of creation against dissolution.

In the last piece he wrote Lawrence, reviewing a book by Eric Gill, quoted with approval Gill's opinion that in a free state a man would do as he liked in his working time, and what was required of him in his spare time; for to work well is to be in 'a state of absorption into the creative spirit, which is God' (P. I. 395). Such would be the condition of freedom, in an England reborn into a right consciousness of the universe, by the restoration of the primary creativity of the phallic consciousness. Eternity inheres in the productions of time; it is achieved in the life of the individual consciousness. All Lawrence's temporal projections—his

Third Age—are therefore, in the last analysis, allegories of personal regeneration, rather than historical prophecies. That is why he is not disconfirmed by the obstinate continuance of the last days, the accelerated ruin of his countryside, the stubborn non-appearance of his Holy Ghost. The 'bad time' prophesied by Mellors came, and stayed. Lawrence's remedy—that men should die into a new life—is no easier now than in his own day, and it is evident that he did not really expect it to be. And at this level alone he is a failed prophet : the lesson, even if it is right, is too hard.

Epilogue

Lawrence, suffering pulmonary crises almost throughout his life, lived so close to death that it was never absent from his imagination. The organic world, with which he sought to be identified, presented him with evidence that life—the life, say, of the poppy—is independent of death, that root, stalk and flower have an immortality that transcends death, and inhabit an eternity free of time. 'The living are always living. The present is one and unbreakable. The present is not a fleeting moment.... My immortality lies in being present in life. And the dead have presence in the living. So that the dead are always present in life, here, in the flesh, always.'[1] Similarly, death is a condition that we know in life, and from which we may be reborn; Lawrence's convalescences cannot have been far from his mind when he imagined the initiate of the mysteries as he finally emerged, separate, 'beyond loneliness' like the risen Jesus[2] or the apples in 'The Ship of Death', that fall 'to bruise an exit for themselves'.

It is not surprising that he should have felt himself growing less interested in individuals as temporal phenomena. The gist of his famous letter to Garnett (*C.L.* 281ff., June 5, 1914) is in the rejection of 'the old stable *ego* of the character'. Three years later, with *Women in Love* behind him, he could tell Murry that fiction didn't interest him any more, because 'you can't have fiction without people... I am weary of humanity and human things. One is happy in the thoughts only that transcend humanity' (*C.L.*514). He was soon to begin *The Lost Girl*, so this was an impermanent mood but a recurrent one, reflected in the momentary intemperance of his dealing with real people, whom he normally handled with tact and understanding. Just so he fluctuated between rage at and acceptance of death.

In the same letter to Murry he observed that what interested him more than people was philosophy. By 1917 he had written a good deal of his 'metaphysic'. The importance of the *Sons and Lovers* foreword is now very obvious. Lawrence had not only passed through a critical period in his life—the death of his mother, his own serious illness, his abandonment of 'Miriam' and elopement with Frieda—but written and rewritten *Sons and Lovers* as a means to understand these events. He knew that 'the greatest living experience for every man is his adventure into the woman', as he put it two years later in a letter to Russell (*C.L.* p. 324); that from the embrace of woman 'comes every new action'. And he thought he knew what hindered this good coming to and going from the woman; it was woman herself as mother, as usurper of the Law and corrupter of sons, banisher of blood-consciousness. He tied this knowledge to his trinitarian scheme, and this told him that love could know the law without becoming its slave, the man know the woman without playing the role of her son. Separateness-in-union could be achieved, if only the Holy Ghost could hold the opposites in tension, keep the man and the woman in an equilibrium beyond the ordinary notion of sexual love.

The maintenance of this separateness came to be the responsibility of the man; the lumbar-sacral ganglia are an image of his separateness, of what prevents him from returning to the navel-consciousness of the child. Hence the growing emphasis on male supremacy, and on male comradeship short of homosexuality. Hence, too, the need to burn out the pride and prudency of women by making them undergo sexual experiences which leave such emotions no place. Here also the triadic or trinitarian scheme prevails, for the reconciler of creative life-flow and shameful, excremental death-flow is the phallus as Holy Ghost, as instrument of initiation into life through ritual death. And another consequence of these convictions was a growing need to change the decadent world by political action—by leadership.

We have seen how this 'philosophy' wrestles with 'art-speech' in the later novels; always ready to follow it to extremes—in 'Education of the People' and *Fantasia*, for example—Lawrence keenly understood that the purpose of fiction was to qualify or even undermine it. This was a matter he thought about intensely throughout his career; and ultimately he solved the problem by seeing the work of art as that third force, the reconciler of opposites, this time story and metaphysic.

The Reconciler was not always equally effective, especially when the recommendations of the metaphysic grew too specific, as in *Kangaroo*. In *Women in Love*, and sometimes in his last years—when he again admitted 'tenderness' to his narrative—Lawrence got the tension he was always seeking. 'Life is so made that opposites sway about a trembling centre of balance.... And of all the art forms the novel most of all demands the trembling and oscillating of the balance' (*P.I.* 529). That is why 'the novel is the book of life' (*C.L.* 535). And it is also why the great novelists have a philosophy that may be 'directly opposite to their passional inspiration' (*P. II.* 417) and why we listen to the novel, not the novelist, who may be 'a dribbling liar'.

If we ask whether it is the art or the 'philosophy' of Lawrence that has kept him alive and meaningful, the answer must be his art, though that is a product of the tension between the intellectual and the passional. And of course the intellectual was a recommendation, an endorsement of the passional. He wanted to tell people how to live. He claimed to have won new freedom for writers (*N. III.* 275: 'It was I who set about smashing down the barriers') and to have done so in order to improve the quality of life. He was disgusted, he told Rhys Davies, with the young, who tolerated 'the impositions of the old world, the old taboos and the mongrel trashy contacts of the civilisation they were forced into.... Your chance is now' (*N*. 271–2). He wanted a world in which people could live, and experience a quickness like his own. And the way to this was by valid sexual relationships, the Holy Ghost presiding over the union of separate bloodstreams. Sexual completeness is the great victory over death, not because it produces new individuals but because it gives access to that immortality which is eternally in the present.

It is easy to disapprove of Lawrence's practical recommendations—he was a male chauvinist (though he believed that woman was the source of value, and that her original corruption into intellect was the work of man) and held views close to Fascist (though he saw through Fascism when it came). Nor would he have approved of the ways in which the tabus have been smashed; promiscuity, the use of others as instruments of self-gratification, always shocked him; he hated pornography and disapproved of divorce. He would have said that we have nothing but a base parody of the new world he had urged into being. The last word on this belongs to Aldous Huxley :

> Here ... let me remark on the fact that Lawrence's doctrine is constantly invoked by people, of whom Lawrence himself would have passionately disapproved, in defence of a behaviour, which he would have found deplorable or even revolting. That this should have happened is by no means, of course, a condemnation of the doctrine. The same philosophy of life may be good or bad according as the person who accepts it and lives by it is intrinsically fine or base ... To the preacher of a new way of life the most depressing thing that can happen is, surely, success. For success permits him to see how those he has converted distort and debase and make ignoble parodies of his teaching.[3]

Lawrence would have been surprised to hear the bishops testify to his morality in the witness-box at the Old Bailey; but he would hardly have thought this enough, and though he might have found something to commend in the ways in which we have altered our lives it seems likely that his reaction to the whole scene would be one of rage: *'Canaille!'* as he liked to shout. His success, such as it has been, would have depressed him: the times, on any view he could possibly have held of them, are still bad.

Chronology

1885	D. H. Lawrence born at Eastwood, Nottinghamshire.
1898–1901	Attended Nottingham High School.
1901	Met Jessie Chambers ('Miriam').
1902–6	Student teacher.
1904	Engaged to Jessie Chambers.
1906	First poems.
1906	Entered University College, Nottingham. Began *The White Peacock* (finished 1910, published 1911).
1907	First stories.
1908	Awarded teacher's certificate at Nottingham U.C.; went to teach in Croydon.
1910	Began *The Trespasser* (pubd. 1912). Broke with Jessie; became engaged to Louie Burrows; began *Paul Morel* (later *Sons and Lovers*, pubd. 1913). Death of mother.
1912	Illness: abandoned teaching career; returned to Eastwood; met Frieda von Richthofen Weekley, and eloped with her to Germany and Italy. Stories; poems pubd. in *Look! We Have Come Through* (1917), *The Widowing of Mrs Holroyd* (1914). Finished *Sons and Lovers*.
1913	Began *The Lost Girl* (*The Insurrection of Miss Houghton*). First versions of essays in *Twilight in Italy* (1916). Began *The Sisters* (first version of *Women in Love* and *The Rainbow*). Wrote 'The Prussian Officer', title story of volume pubd. 1914.
1914	Returned to England in June. Wrote *Thomas Hardy*, worked on *The Sisters*.
1915	*The Rainbow* published and suppressed. Friendship with Russell. Wrote 'The Crown'. Tried to get passports for U.S.A.
1916	Cornwall. Quarrel with Russell. Wrote *Women in Love*.

1917   Wrote 'The Reality of Peace'. Began *Studies in Classic American Literature*. Was refused passports. Failed army medical examination. Persecuted by the army and expelled from Cornwall on suspicion of spying. Began *Aaron's Rod* (pubd. 1922).

1918   Wrote most of *Movements in European Literature* (1921). Play *Touch and Go*. 'Education of the People'. First version of *The Fox* (1923). Army medical examination described in *Kangaroo*.

1919   Stories for *England My England*; finished first draft *Aaron's Rod*. Went to Italy.

1920   Lived in Florence, Capri, and Taormina, Sicily. Sicilian poems of *Birds, Beasts and Flowers* (1923). Revised *S.C.A.L.* Finished *The Lost Girl*, worked on *Aaron's Rod*. Wrote *Psychoanalysis and the Unconscious* (1921) and fragmentary novel *Mr. Noon*.

1921   Visit to Sardinia, and wrote *Sea and Sardinia* (1921). *Fantasia of the Unconscious* (1922). Final version *Aaron's Rod*; *The Captain's Doll* and *The Ladybird*.

1922   Translating Sicilian novelist Verga; introduction to Maurice Magnus's *Memoirs of the Foreign Legion* (1924). Left for Ceylon, where the Lawrences stayed with the Brewsters; arrived in Australia in May. Wrote most of *Kangaroo* (1923). Arrived in Taos, New Mexico. Rewrote Mollie Skinner's *The Boy in the Bush* (1924).

1923   More of *Birds, Beasts and Flowers*. Final version of *S.C.A.L.* (1923). First draft *Plumed Serpent* (1926). Visited Mexico. Visited England and Europe.

1924   Saw Frederick Carter in Shropshire. Returned to Taos. Wrote pieces for *Mornings in Mexico* (1927). *The Woman Who Rode Away* (pubd. 1928). *St Mawr* (1925). *The Princess*. Began revision of *Quetzalcoatl* (*The Plumed Serpent*, 1926).

1925   Seriously ill in Mexico City. *The Flying Fish*. Final version *Plumed Serpent*. The play *David*. Essays on the novel. Returned to England, then to Germany and Italy.

1926   *The Virgin and the Gipsy* (1930). Stories. Settled in Villa Mirenda, near Florence. Last visit to England.

Began *Lady Chatterley's Lover* (1928), wrote first two versions.

1927   Paintings. First part of *Escaped Cock* (*The Man Who Died*, 1929). Correspondence with Trigant Burrow. Began *Etruscan Places* (1932).

1928   Final version *L.C.L.* Visit to Germany. Lived at Bandol, in South of France. Manuscript of *Pansies* seized by postal authorities. Finished *The Man Who Died*. Many articles; 'Introduction to These Paintings'.

1929   Visit to Majorca; Florence, Germany: return to Bandol. Seizure of paintings in London. *More Pansies* (1932). *My Skirmish with Jolly Roger* (later enlarged as *A Propos of Lady Chatterley's Lover* (1930)). *Nettles* (1930). *Pornography and Obscenity* (1929). *Apocalypse* (1931).

1930   Moved into sanatorium at Vence, 6 February. Died 2 March.

Short Bibliography

(Abbreviated titles used in the text are given in parentheses after the entry)

PRINCIPAL WORKS OF LAWRENCE

(Dates of first publication followed by current editions, paperback when possible)

(A) NOVELS

The White Peacock, 1911. (Penguin). (*W.P.*)
The Trespasser, 1912. (Penguin). (*T.*)
Sons and Lovers, 1913. (Penguin; Viking Press) See also *Sons and Lovers: Text, Background and Criticism*, ed. Julian Moynahan, Viking Critical Library). (*S.L.*)
The Rainbow, 1915. (Penguin; Viking). (*R.*)
Women in Love, 1920. (Penguin; Viking). (*W.L.*)
The Lost Girl, 1920. (Penguin; Viking). (*L.G.*)
Aaron's Rod, 1922. (Penguin; Viking). (*A.R.*)
Kangaroo, 1924. (Penguin; Viking). (K.)
The Boy in the Bush (with M. L. Skinner) 1924. (Penguin). (*B.B.*)
The Plumed Serpent, 1926. (Penguin; Viking). (*P.S.*)
Lady Chatterley's Lover, 1928. (Penguin; Viking). (*L.C.L.*)
[The two earlier versions are published as *The First Lady Chatterley* (1972) and *John Thomas and Lady Jane* (1972)]

(B) SHORTER FICTION

Lawrence's short stories are published complete in three volumes by Viking. The Penguin collections *Love Among the Haystacks, England My England, The Woman Who Rode Away,*

The Prussian Officer, The Princess and *The Mortal Coil* together include all the short stories.

For the novelle, Viking's *Four Short Novels of D.H.L.* includes *Love Among the Haystacks, The Ladybird, The Fox* and *The Captain's Doll*. Penguin's *Love Among the Haystacks* includes, along with the title story and some short stories, *The Man Who Died; The Ladybird* (Penguin) includes the novella of that title, with *The Fox* and *The Captain's Doll; St Mawr* and *The Virgin and the Gipsy* share a volume.

(C) PLAYS

The Complete Plays of D. H. Lawrence (Heinemann, 1965, Viking, 1966).

(D) POEMS

The Complete Poems of D. H. Lawrence, ed. Vivian De Sola Pinto and F. Warren Roberts (Heinemann, Viking, 1964). (*C.P.*) Penguin has a *Selected Poems* with introduction by W. E. Williams (1950), Viking a *Selected Poems*, introduction by Kenneth Rexroth (1959).

(E) TRAVEL

Twilight in Italy, 1916. (Penguin; Viking).
Sea and Sardinia, (Penguin; Viking).
Mornings in Mexico, 1927. (Penguin, in one volume with following title). *Etruscan Places*, 1932. (Penguin, with *Mornings in Mexico*; Viking singly).

(F) OTHER PROSE

Phoenix: The Posthumous Papers of D. H. Lawrence, ed. Edward D. McDonald, 1936. (Heinemann; Viking). (*P.I.*)
Phoenix II: More Uncollected Writings, ed. Warren Roberts and Harry T. Moore, 1968. (Heinemann; Viking). (*P.II.*)

These volumes contain, among other essays, 'Pornography and Obscenity', 'Study of Thomas Hardy', 'John Galsworthy', 'Introduction to These Paintings', 'Education of the People', 'The Reality of Peace', 'Prologue to *Women in Love*', 'The Crown' (originally published in *Reflections on the Death of a Porcu-*

pine (1925), essays on the novel, and such important brief pieces as 'The State of Funk' and 'The Risen Lord'.

Movements in European History (by 'Lawrence H. Davison'), 1921. 2nd ed. of 1925 under D.H.L.'s name. New edition with previously unpublished afterword, Oxford University Press, 1972.

Psychoanalysis and the Unconscious, 1921; *Fantasia and the Unconscious*, 1922. Published together with introduction by Philip Rieff, Viking Compass.

Studies in Classic American Literature, 1923. (Viking Compass.) The earlier versions of these essays published as *The Symbolic Meaning*, ed. Armin Arnold, 1962. (*S.C.A.L.*)

Pornography and Obscenity, 1929. (In *Phoenix I*; and see next item.)

A Propos of Lady Chatterley's Lover, 1930 (first version, *My Skirmish With Jolly Roger*, 1929). (In *Phoenix II*; also reprinted, with *Pornography and Obscenity*, the 'Introduction to *Pansies*', and other relevant pieces, in *Sex, Literature and Censorship*, ed. Harry T. Moore (Viking Compass).

Apocalypse, 1931. (Viking Compass.)

Penguin publish *Selected Essays* and a selection from *Phoenix*. There is a *Selected Literary Criticism*, ed. Anthony Beal (Mercury).

(G) LETTERS

The Letters of D.H. Lawrence, ed. Aldous Huxley, 1932. (This collection is out of print, but contains important material – e.g., the Foreword to *Sons and Lovers* – not included in the next item. The introductory essay of Huxley is reprinted in the next item).

The Collected Letters of D. H. Lawrence, ed. Harry T. Moore, 1962 (Heinemann; Viking). (*C.L.*)

(H) SELECTION

The Portable D. H. Lawrence, ed. Diana Trilling (Viking).

(I) BIBLIOGRAPHY

Warren Roberts, *A Bibliography of D. H. Lawrence*, 1963.

BOOKS ABOUT LAWRENCE

(A) BIOGRAPHY

Harry T. Moore, *The Intelligent Heart*, 1954. (Penguin.)
Edward Nehls, *D. H. Lawrence: A Composite Biography* (three volumes, 1957, 1958, 1959).   (N. I, II, III)

(B) CRITICISM

(As in (A) great quantities of material are omitted; only what strikes the present writer as of high value is mentioned.)
Colin Clarke, *River of Dissolution*, 1969.
H. M. Dalewski, *The Forked Flame*, 1965.
George H. Ford, *Double Measure*, 1965.
John Goode, 'D. H. Lawrence', in *The Twentieth Century* (Sphere History of English Literature, Volume 7, ed. Bernard Bergonzi, 1970) pp. 106–52.
Graham Hough, *The Dark Sun*, 1956. (Penguin.)
F. R. Leavis, *D. H. Lawrence, Novelist*, 1955. (Penguin.)
K. Sagar, *The Art of D. H. Lawrence*, 1966. (In paper.)
Mark Kinkead Weekes, 'The Marble and the Statue' in *Imagined Worlds, Essays. . . . in Honour of John Butt*, ed. Maynard Mack and Ian Gregor, 1968, pp. 371–418.
D. H. Lawrence: The Critical Heritage, ed. R. P. Draper, 1970.

Notes

PROLOGUE (pages 7–23)

1. *Lady Chatterley's Lover*, XI.
2. 'E.T.' (Jessie Chambers), *D. H. Lawrence: A Personal Record*, 1935, p. 117.
3. Graham Hough, *The Dark Sun* (1956, Penguin ed. 1961, pp. 44 and 48–9).
4. There is an excellent study of Lawrence's Wagnerian interests in William Blissett's 'D. H. Lawrence, D'Annunzio, Wagner', *Contemporary Literature*, vii (1966), pp. 21–46.
5. Dorothy Van Ghent, *The English Novel: Form and Function* (1953) pp. 245–61; reprinted, with other excellent critical material on this novel, in D. H. Lawrence : *Sons and Lovers; Text, Background, and Criticism*, ed. Julian Moynahan (Viking Critical Library), 1968, pp. 527–46.
6. Louis L. Martz, 'Portrait of Miriam', in *Imagined Worlds: Essays on some English Novels and Novelists in Honour of John Butt*, ed. Maynard Mack and Ian Gregor, 1968, p. 351.
7. *L.C.L.* VIII.
8. Simon O. Lesser, *Fiction and the Unconscious*, 1957, pp. 175–78.
9. Philip Rieff, 'Two Honest Men', *The Listener* LXIII (May 5, 1960), reprinted in *Sons and Lovers: Text, Background and Criticism*, pp. 518–26.

ONE 1913–1917 (pages 25–75)

1. *Fantasia of the Unconscious* (1922) in *Psychoanalysis and the Unconscious* and *Fantasia of the Unconscious*, introduction by Philip Rieff, 1960, p. 57.
2. Ezra Pound, letter of March 1913 to Harriet Monroe (*Letters*, ed. D. D. Paige, 1951, p. 52).
3. *Letters of D. H. Lawrence*, ed. Aldous Huxley, 1932, pp. 95–102.

4. 'The Marble and the Statue', in *Imagined Worlds, Essays on Some English Novels and Novelists in Honour of John Butt*, ed. Maynard Mack and Ian Gregor (1968) pp. 371–418. There is more work to be done on the Texas MSS, especially on the material relating to *Women in Love*, and it is certain that we shall find out more about the chronology of composition.

5. Harry T. Moore, *The Intelligent Heart* (1955, Penguin ed. revised, 1960), p. 254.

6. F. R. Leavis, *D. H. Lawrence, Novelist* (1955, Penguin ed. 1964) p. 148.

7. Moore, op. cit., p. 231.

8. 'The Marble and the Statue', p. 400.

9. op. cit., p. 401.

10. Emile Delavenay, *D. H. Lawrence: L'Homme et la Genèse de son Oeuvre: Les Années de Formation, 1885–1919* (Paris, 1969), p. 350. An English version of this book appeared in 1972 (*D. H. Lawrence: The Man and His Work*. London: Heinemann).

11. *Twilight in Italy*, III.

12. See Norman Cohn, *The Pursuit of the Millennium* (1957, 3rd ed. revised, 1970).

13. By this he meant the Protestant theology of history, which prophesied increasing corruption until at the climax anti-Christ would appear in the last days. For a study of this and other aspects of Joachitism, see Frank E. Manuel, *Shapes of Philosophical History* (1965). Other works dealing with the history of Joachitism are Norman Cohn, *The Pursuit of the Millennium* (1957, 3rd edition revised, 1970) and A. L. Morton, *The Everlasting Gospel* (1958). Lawrence discusses the Joachite doctrines in *Movements in European History*; the direct source of his information is unknown. Any encyclopaedia gives some of the facts, but Joachitism was enshrined in much occultism.

14. Houston Stewart Chamberlain, *Foundations of the Nineteenth Century*, translated by John Lees (1913), I. xcvi.

15. *Foundations*, I. 401.

16. Delavenay, *D. H. Lawrence*, 286 ff.

17. Delavenay, *D. H. Lawrence*, 327 ff.

18. See Gilbert Seldes, *The Stamering Century* (1928, ed. of 1965), p. 183.

19. *D. H. Lawrence and Edward Carpenter: A Study in Edwardian Transition* (1971). See also Samuel Hynes, *The Edwardian Turn of Mind* (1968).

20. These reviews were by Evelyn Scott in *The Dial,* an anonym in *Saturday Westminster Gazette,* and Middleton Murry in *The Nation and Athenaeum;* reprinted in R. P. Draper, *D. H. Lawrence: The Critical Heritage* (1970), pp. 162, 167, 172.

21. J. Middleton Murry, *Reminiscences of D. H. Lawrence* (1933), p. 247.

22. *Reminiscences,* p. 103.

23. Full text in Draper, *Critical Heritage,* pp. 343–7.

24. Richard Hoggart, quoted in *The Completed Poems of D. H. Lawrence,* ed. V. De Sola Pinto and F. Warren Roberts (1964), p. 15.

25. 'In a novel, everything is relative to everything else, if that novel is art at all. There may be didactic bits, but they aren't the novel' (*P.*II 416).

TWO 1917–21 (pages 76–98)

1. Moore, *Intelligent Heart,* p. 288 (not in *C.L.*).

2. *C.P.* I.259.

3. *C.P.* I. 266–7.

4. 'Lawrence H. Davison', *Movements in European History* (1921, new ed. 1925), p. 344. In 1925 Lawrence wrote, for a new edition, an Epilogue which remained unpublished until 1972 (*Movements in European History,* ed. J. T. Boulton). It is an harangue on the separateness of the races, and their power to develop or to decline. The war destroyed Europe's power to grow – hence all the subsequent disorders, Socialism giving rise to Fascism ('only another kind of bullying'). Lawrence urges the boys and girls to seek out a natural nobility in themselves, for this must replace the ruined hereditary aristocracy and restore order to nations.

5. *Movements,* p. 194.

6. *D. H. Lawrence, Novelist,* p. 156.

7. *D. H. Lawrence, Novelist,* pp. 206–34.

THREE 1922–1925 (pages 99–114)

1. Michael Wilding, 'Between Scylla and Charybdis: *Kangaroo* and the Form of the Political Novel', *Australian Literary Studies*, IV (1970), p. 335.
2. The Penguin edition (p. 71) reads 'we are as California. . . .', which can hardly be right.
3. Draper, *Critical Heritage*, pp. 265–71.
4. Hough, *The Dark Sun*, pp. 211 ff.

FOUR 1925–1930 (pages 115–39)

1. All three versions are now in print (see Bibliography) and provide material for closer study of Lawrence's remarkable assiduity in rewriting. Even in the parts he decided to leave substantially unchanged he made innumerable verbal alterations; scarcely a single sentence is repeated *verbatim*. The first version is the shortest and the simplest. It is much more interested in the class difference between Connie and her lover than the later ones, and although the story is not very different in outline it is possible to see that Lawrence, as he reworked it, needed more incident, more characters and more doctrinal intrusions. The second version is unsatisfactory, losing the simplicity of the first without attaining the fullness of the third. If the third version is in some ways the shrillest it is also undoubtedly the strongest, the most fully realised. It is the product of an energetic refining process, and the full significance of Lawrence's text emerges only at the end after being twice reimagined.
2. Introduction to *Pansies*, *C.P.* p. 240.
3. See G. W. Knight, 'Lawrence, Joyce and Powys', *Essays in Criticism* XI (1961) and in *Neglected Powers* (1971); J. Sparrow, 'Regina vs. Penguin Books', *Encounter*, 101 (1962), pp. 35–43; F. Kermode, 'Spenser and the Allegorists', (British Academy Warton Lecture, 1962, reprinted in *Shakespeare, Spenser, Donne*, 1971); George Ford, *Double Measure* (1965); Colin Clarke, *River of Dissolution* (1969); Mark Spilka, 'Lawrence Up-Tight', *Novel* IV (1971), pp. 252–67; Ford, Kermode, Clarke, Spilka, 'Critical Exchange', *Novel* V (1971), pp. 54–70.

4. Conveniently gathered in Harry T. Moore's collection, *D. H. Lawrence: Sex, Literature and Censorship* (Viking Compass, 1953). This book has a useful introduction recounting Lawrence's dealing with censorship from the prosecution of *The Rainbow* to the suppression of *Lady Chatterley's Lover* and *Pansies,* and the seizure of his paintings at the Warren Gallery in 1929.

5. Moore, *Intelligent Heart,* p. 94.

6. *C.P.,* p. 444.

7. 'Pax', *C.P.,* p. 700.

NOTES TO EPILOGUE (pages 140–4)

1. *The Symbolic Meaning,* p. 78.

2. *The Man Who Died.*

3. *Letters* of *D. H. Lawrence,* ed. Aldous Huxley, 1932, p. xiii.

Fontana Books

Fontana is at present best known (outside the field of popular fiction) for its extensive list of books on history, philosophy and theology. Now, however, the list is expanding rapidly to include most main subjects, such as literature, politics, economics and sociology. At the same time, the number of paperback reprints of books already published in hardcover editions is being increased. Further information on Fontana's present list and future plans can be obtained from: The Non-Fiction Editor, Fontana Books, 14 St James's Place, London S.W.1.

All Fontana books are available at your bookshop or newsagent; or can be ordered direct. Just fill in the form below and list the titles you want.

....

FONTANA BOOKS, Cash Sales Department, P.O. Box 4, Godalming, Surrey. Please send purchase price plus 5p postage per book by cheque, postal or money order. No currency.

NAME (Block Letters) _____

ADDRESS _____

_____

_____

Fontana Social Science

Books available include:

African Genesis   Robert Ardrey   **50p**

The Territorial Imperative   Robert Ardrey   **50p**

Racial Minorities   Michael Banton   **50p**

The Sociology of Modern Britain
Edited by Eric Butterworth and David Weir   **60p**

Social Problems of Modern Britain
Edited by Eric Butterworth and David Weir   **75p**

Strikes   Richard Hyman   **50p**

Memories, Dreams, Reflections   C. J. Jung   **60p**

Strike at Pilkingtons   Tony Lane and Kenneth Roberts   **50p**

Figuring Out Society   Ronald Meek   **45p**

Lectures on Economic Principles   Sir Dennis Robertson   **75p**

People and Cities   Stephen Verney   **37½p**

Fontana Literature